Fred T

MW00638810

10 Essential Skills of
Executive Leadership
Series

FOUNDATIONS FOR
SELF-LEADERSHIP

Fred T. Garmon, Ph.D.

FOUNDATIONS FOR SELF-LEADERSHIP

ISBN: 978-1-64288-250-6

Fred T. Garmon, Ph.D.

Dedicated to

Bill George
Bob Pace
Don Anderson
Pam Adams
Ted Jones
and my wife,
Shirley Jones Garmon

10 Essential Skills
of Executive Leadership

Principles & Presuppositions:
Foundations for Self-Leadership

1. Integrity of Heart

2. Self-Awareness

3. Servant Leadership

4. Situational Leadership

5. Transformational Leadership

6. Leading Change

7. Managing Conflict

8. Water You Swim In

9. The Road Ahead

10. Developing a Bench

Fred T. Garmon, Ph.D.

FOUNDATIONS FOR
SELF-LEADERSHIP
-GETTING STARTED-

TABLE OF CONTENTS

Fred T. Garmon, Ph.D.

"CHASE THE RABBITS"

Throughout this book and the entire series, you'll come across this **"RABBIT"** icon. The icon refers to the urban dictionary informal phrase depicting an *IDEA* - "Chasing a rabbit".

"Chasing a rabbit" *usually* means doing something totally irrelevant or getting distracted from what you were intending to do or accomplish—getting side-tracked.

But I'm turning the idea on its head and want to encourage you to TAKE TIME and PLAN to *"chase certain rabbits"* (concepts, theories, ideas, terms), that I draw your attention to, in order to gain deeper and more substantive understanding of the material.

A Message from Dr. Bill George
(*1941-2017*) *mentor and friend*

CONGRATULATIONS!

If you are holding this book in your hands, it means you have taken a bold, courageous step in the right direction. You have decided to learn about leadership in order to become a better, more effective leader.

It might surprise you to realize how relatively few people commit themselves to this kind of enterprise. It is as if they think they already know all they need to know to be able to set direction, cast vision, supervise, reach goals, develop teams, and keep their followers committed and working in harmony.

And how did they acquire this knowledge and these skills? Evidently, by osmosis. That's a biology term that originally meant the ability of a liquid (usually water) to pass through the walls of a living cell. It has come to mean an ability to learn and understand things gradually without much effort.

One of my seminary classmates told me he slept with his Greek book under his pillow. Frankly, I doubt that helped much! Although any man or woman should be commended for attempting to learn by observing and copying an example, mastering the subject of leadership usually requires a competent teacher and an exceptional curriculum, matched with a personal investment of time and effort.

If you are looking for practical and proven ways to improve your effectiveness a leader, you are in the right place, with the right book in your hand. Fred Garmon is not just another leadership professor; he is a leadership practitioner. He lives in the arena of leadership realities, not just leadership theories.

You are engaging in a great adventure, one that will enhance your personal efficacy and equip you to develop other leaders, which—at heart—is one of the principal tasks of any leader.

Blessings upon you as you learn, grow, and lead!
Dr. Bill George

WELCOME

to **LeaderLabs** and to **the 10 Essential Skills Executive Leadership** program.

Peter Drucker, *the father of modern management told us, "We are living in an age of social transformation out of which will come a world that will be different from anything anyone today imagines."*

As a leader yourself, you know that leadership is changing and you need to stay on top of the latest strategies to lead—and succeed in ministry or the marketplace. LeaderLabs strive to present you with fresh perspectives—enabling you to prepare for the opportunities and challenges ahead.

Participants in our LeaderLabs 10 Essential Skills of Executive Leadership (10ES ELP) or any of my other leadership programs, will gain new perspectives and develop a solid foundation upon which to build a successful and effective future. Persons who take part learn how to focus on why they are doing what they're doing, how to do it better, and how to develop a realistic, motivational plan for achieving their goals.

This book and entire program are, therefore, filled with information, knowledge, and wisdom from management gurus, contemporary entrepreneurs and dynamic millennial leaders—sifted through the filter of scripture, ministry and marketplace experience. The program will, hopefully, challenge you and stimulate spirited thought and discussion—inspiring positive change and new levels of excellence.

I'd like you to think of this book as a short, intensive seminar. Use it for personal development and to develop your leadership team. My hope is that the lessons will help to challenge conventional solutions and encourage you to think beyond old boundaries or "old wineskins."

I congratulate you on taking the first steps toward a new future you—one that is more effective and more intentional.

I look forward to our journey together.

Fred T. Garmon, Ph.D.
Executive Director, Founder
LeaderLabs, Inc.

SECTION 1

LET'S
SET
THE
STAGE

WHY THIS BOOK and THIS SERIES?

It has been observed that the only constant in the world today over the past few decades has been change. Change will continue. Citizens in the 21st century will be confronted with increasingly complex ministerial, social, cultural, economic, technological and global challenges. This season we now find ourselves in is being referred to by the acronym V.U.C.A.

VOLATILITY   UNCERTAINTY   COMPLEXITY   AMBIGUITY

LEADING IN A VUCA WORLD

The complexity of these issues will defy understanding and coping without the ability to integrate knowledge and transfer it to others within diverse and dynamic contexts.

Leadership development programs are, therefore, also faced with increasingly difficult challenges. Ministerial development and Christian formation programs must also take this reality seriously.

Leaders will thus need to be **flexible, autonomous, collaborative, and adaptable** if they are to deal with the exponential growth of information and ubiquitous change.

In a world that is constantly changing, why should we ever stop learning?

Such complex problems need to be addressed by individuals who possess sophisticated, diversified and complementary competencies. The ability to train "on the fly," engaging short, substantive, job and ministry specific knowledge and experience will be indispensable.

"Training on the fly will be indispensable – Competency Based, Certificate and Nanolearning."

Competency-based training will be short-term, job and/or ministry specific, context-particular learning, based on benchmarked skills needed for effective leadership and superior performance. *LeaderLabs 3.0 is designed as competency-based training for ministry development.*

Certificate-based training could be as short as a half-hour video or as involved as a multi-course program taking six months or more. A training certificate is typically awarded after a student has completed a certificate-based course. *LeaderLabs' programs are typically eight-day programs; two days a month for four months.*

Nanolearning is the future of learning

Nanolearning is a growing learning modality or idea, delivering condensed information in an engaging format. It provides a few soundbites or sentences of valuable and relevant content via platforms like Tik Tok, Twitter or YouTube. The term is also used to signify a new type of short-term degree that people seek and acquire during their working or ministry lifetime.

A Nano-Degree is a course of study much shorter than a university program and one that focuses on specific skills and competencies needed for relevant and immediate application. Nanolearning is often received as bits and pieces of information in an entertaining and engaging way.

Generation Z (1997-2012) is already learning more from short soundbites on Snapchat, Tik Tok and YouTube than from textbooks and other training methods. As the first generation to grow up with smartphones, many of their learning methodologies will be unrecognizable from previous generations.

We have to rethink teachers, content, credentials, assessments, resources, technologies and locations. How we learn, where we get that learning from, and how we know we've learned, will never be the same.

Teachers and professors will continue to play essential roles in our society — but in a different way. With the volume of information online, teachers will become master curators. They'll learn quickly, be flexible and instruct their students effectively with the most relevant content.

LeaderLabs, therefore, seeks to address this need for Christian leaders—what I see as **competencies, *concepts, and principles, that are supplemental* to normal ministerial and theological training.**

So, let's begin unpacking the 10 Essential Skills of Executive Leadership Program.

I begin by stating **what the program is not** and then by clearly stating my bias in regards to the choice of program content.

- The LeaderLabs 10ES Executive Leadership Program **does not** attempt to duplicate or compete with seminary or theological education. Seminary and Bible School education is foundational to the work and ministry of a minister. I find myself, however, agreeing with R. Fowler White, the Dean of Faculty and Professor of New Testament at Knox Theological Seminary. *"Theological education is necessary, but it is not sufficient for effectiveness in ministry."*

  I have believed this for a long time, but was not willing to admit it. *Theological and ministerial education only addresses about 30% of the skill base needed for ministry and marketplace ministry in the 21st century.*

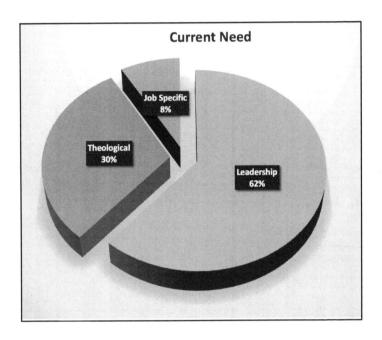

- The 10 Essentials program **DOES NOT** attempt to present a comprehensive review or summary of every stream of research that touches the subject of leadership.

I admit **my bias** and state upfront that I have made judgments about the relevance and importance in deciding what material to cover and include in this program.

These judgments were not, however, made haphazardly, but have been based on my years of study and continuous review of. academic materials, articles, books, seminars, and conferences spanning multiple applicable disciplines.

The content selections are also influenced by my educational experience in the fields of theology and organizational leadership which have been integrated into more than 40 years of experience in the full-time ministry; both within the USA and on the mission field.

The content additionally has been informed by years of teaching, training, researching and consulting.

And finally, the 10 Essentials program content has been and continues to be reviewed by colleagues who share my passion for leadership development.

- My goal is to present the most relevant findings from all pertinent silos, with a focus on information that can be implemented, acted on, and utilized in day-to-day faith-based leadership circumstances.

The 10 Essentials of Executive Leadership Program is first and foremost a process oriented, developmental journey that utilizes "learning LABS" for an engaging, thought-provoking, and fun learning experience. It is designed to take ministry and marketplace leadership to the next level and into a life-long learning practice.

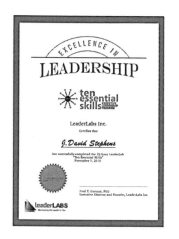

The 10ES Executive Leadership program, along with this book, which is part of that program, is *a*

**certificate level,
Nano-degree
leadership program**

designed to expose Christian leaders and managers to next-level leadership concepts and to encourage a safe learning community that will:

- Ignite a passion to learn,
- Provide valid and reliable, confidential feedback,
- Encourage immediate application of what is learned, and
- Inspire participants to impart to others what is learned.

Many leaders do the right things intuitively, but do not know how to articulate the process appropriately. The 10ES Executive Leadership program will provide the supplemental vocabulary that will enable leaders to understand and express *natural and acquired* behaviors at a new level.

Every one of us has an equal opportunity—
- The opportunity to make a difference,
- The opportunity to be ALL we can be.

I cannot be you. But I can be the BEST ME I can be!
We each have one opportunity and *THIS is it*.

You may be engaging this material in a classroom setting with other colleagues or within the privacy of your own sacred study, but the one thing we have in common is that we are becoming part of an army of trained men and women, committed to excellence in leadership.

We are, therefore, in these changing and opportunistic times, committed

- To the gaining and integration of knowledge,
- To the creation of intentional teams of colleagues, and
- To the sharing and transference of this knowledge to others within dynamic and diverse contexts.

So let the development begin.

LEADERS, born or made? But especially made.

Leadership is one of *the* **most observed phenomena.** It is universally recognized and acknowledged, but difficult to define. But, ask any member of a local congregation or organizational team and they will tell you when they see it and when they don't.

A mystique has existed about leaders for millennia, as well as a fascination with explaining leadership.

- Where do leaders come from?
- Are they born under some lucky star?
- How are leaders defined?
- What characterizes good leaders?
- How do leaders persuade people to follow them?
- What is it about *good* leaders that make them different from others?

- Are they born with hard-to-duplicate qualities that enable them to make better decisions, generate better performances, and get better results than anyone else?
- Or is there a set of fundamental skills for effective leadership that, when taught, absorbed, and practiced, can make a significant difference to any individual and any organization?

There is no simple, cookie-cutter answer to these important questions but I believe they can be summed up by the words, **"It Depends."** *More on this concept later.*

This one thing is certain however. **All leadership is context sensitive** and especially so considering the changing, challenging and exciting times we find ourselves living in today. So, we have to think; and think hard. And we have to once again regain a love for learning—for being the best me, the best you, that we can possibly become. Now that's a goal worth committing to! **To be <u>ALL</u> YOU CAN BE.**

I am excited, therefore, about the possibilities for training ministry leaders, but I also see clearly the leadership crisis that is prevalent all around us in the market place and ministry. And it is a staggering problem; especially so when we realize that valid research states that between 15,000 to 50,000 ministers leave the ministry every year, a figure that does not include collateral damage or silent deaths—family and community members or those who leave but never notify anyone officially.

Stevie Smith's poem sums it up, entitled,

"Not Waving, But Drowning."

The poem represents the interior monologue of a drowned man, trying, even in death to convey to the living his long journey of desperation.

For this man, ministry was a grim and ugly premise. And sadly, many in ministry today, declare the same testimony of desperately needing help while everyone around them seems to be misunderstanding their calls for support.

This is where I found myself after 30+ years of ministry. Decades of ministry experience, having completed undergraduate and Master of Divinity work—struggling through a PhD in Leadership, while pastoring.

I was drowning and did not know where to turn. It was while being immersed in doctoral studies that I vividly remember leaning back in my chair and saying out loud, **"Where has** *this stuff* **been?"**

"This stuff" was practical information about the manner in which corporate executives were being developed and the skills that were being emphasized to them, as "essential." The corporate world was spending billions of dollars every year developing skills like *conflict management* and *leading change.* But I had never been provided even basic information about such practical and relevant *learnable* skills.

I had earned my undergraduate degree in Biblical Studies, my Master of Divinity degree from seminary, and yet something was missing; further training was needed. It was during my Ph.D. studies in Leadership at Regent University in Virginia Beach, Virginia that I would find much of what was missing and be given the tools for life-long learning.

I made up my mind to seek out the top ten essential skills needed by Christian leaders (especially those in ministry), and give myself to learning and practicing them personally. I also committed myself to developing training programs that could be shared with my colleagues in ministry and with those in any station of Christian leadership.

I had a desire, and passion, to help myself, but also to help others become the best leaders they could possibly be. I wanted to integrate the intellectual data and information, the concepts, theories, and vocabulary I had discovered, into ministerial praxis. This new material would therefore be supplemental material to ministerial training.

I refer to the training concept as **LeaderLabs** and to the specific teachings within **LeaderLabs 1.0**, under the title of the **10 Essential Skills of Executive Leadership.**

ten essential skills
EXECUTIVE LEADERSHIP PROGRAM

1. Principles & Precepts;
   Foundations for Self-Leadership
2. Integrity of Heart
3. Self-Awareness
4. Servant Leadership
5. Situational Leadership
6. Leading Change
7. Managing Conflict
8. Water You Swim In
9. The Road Ahead
10. Developing a Bench

These 10 skills represent what I believe to be the set of fundamental skills for effective leadership, that, when taught, absorbed, and practiced, can and will make a significant difference to any individual, church or organization.

Leadership skills can be learned. Leaders can be made. You can acquire skill sets that enable you to be a better leader. And it's a process not an event. It happens over time. You can't see plants growing—unless you speed up a film—but you know that they do grow. Each day, tiny changes take place. It's the same with your life, ministry and career.

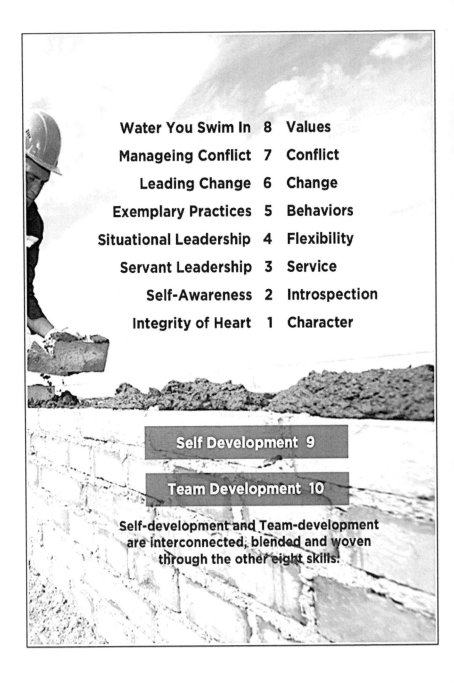

Water You Swim In 8 Values

Manageing Conflict 7 Conflict

Leading Change 6 Change

Exemplary Practices 5 Behaviors

Situational Leadership 4 Flexibility

Servant Leadership 3 Service

Self-Awareness 2 Introspection

Integrity of Heart 1 Character

Self Development 9

Team Development 10

Self-development and Team-development
are interconnected, blended and woven
through the other eight skills.

Leadership Skills Can Be Learned.
Leaders can be made.
FOUNDATIONS FOR SELF-LEADERSHIP
Getting Started

Have you ever asked yourself the question, *"What makes a great leader?"* or *"What skills do I need to become the best leader I can be?"*

We used to talk about the need for **"hard skills."** These were subjects like English, math, science, history, and literature, etc. But today, more than ever before, we are seeing the need for what is referred to as **"soft skills."**

Soft skills, like collaboration, interpersonal awareness, teamwork, conflict management, leadership, leading change, etc. were thought to be secondary to hard skills. But there is nothing soft about struggling at work or ministry to get along with people, feeling like a failure, like you're always playing catchup or flailing in the deep end of the pool.

I believe it's time we referred to these things by what they really are—**ESSENTIAL SKILLS**. How can teamwork and collaboration not be seen as extremely important? I thought I had been absent when they taught these things in college or seminary, but nope, they didn't teach it.

And yet, a Global Talent Trend report showed that 92% of talent professionals and hiring personnel say that soft skills are just as important—or more important than hard skills.

92%

And unlike hard skills, *soft skills* are directly transferable to the job, organization, industry and ministry.

Take **Emotional Intelligence** as an example—having self-awareness and social-awareness is now seen to be twice as important as one's IQ or intelligence quotient. It's said that IQ will get you in the door but EQ, your ability to get along with people, will keep you in the door.

Research by **Daniel Goleman**, psychologist and coauthor of *Emotional Intelligence* and *Primal Leadership*, has shown that emotional intelligence is a more powerful determinant of good leadership than technical competence, IQ, or vision. It is now one of the crucial criteria in hiring, promotions, and performance evaluations.

Emotional Intelligence encompasses both personal competence and social competence. Personal competence is made up of self-awareness and self-management while social competence uses social awareness and relationship management.

Personal competence = Self-Awareness and Self-Management

Social competence = Social-Awareness and Relationship-Management.

So, training is critical. It's not an either-or proposition. We need hard technical skills and soft skills, what I refer to as essential skills. These essential skills should not be overlooked.

The Navy Seals have a saying that represents the importance of this principle.

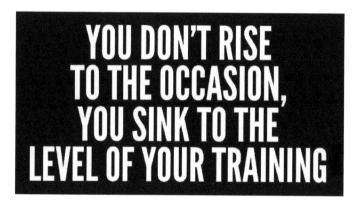

Dr. Henry Cloud is also known for emphasizing this fundamental truth. He says,

> *"You have to develop yourself to where situations do not have power over you. So that when you're in the heat of the moment, you're able to come up with a lot of choices. Your training will provide you with a lot of options. You're able to think and pull from your tool bag."*

Scripture also speaks to this issue. Paul, in **1 Timothy 4:7** says, **"_Train_ yourself to be Godly."** Paul then adds,

"For physical training is of some value, but Godliness has value for all things, holding promise for both the present life and the life to come."

The word **"training"** in the *Greek* language is a derivative of the word "gymnasium." It implies the meaning of an intentional, rigorous, and disciplined process.

Thomas Jefferson said it this way, *"If you want something you've never had, then you have to be willing to do something you've never done."*

A CURATOR OF INFORMATION

This is the first book in a series of books that will fundamentally deal with these questions. The answers come in what I refer to as the **10 Essential Skills of Executive Leadership**. I see myself as a curator of information; gathering intellectual data from diverse disciplines and individuals, pulling it through the filter of scripture, along with ministerial and life experience.

I will, therefore, within the pages of this first book, work to provide **a foundation and philosophical basis** for the 10

Essential Skills and discuss their importance to the Christian leader.

After that, the remaining books in the series will take a deeper look at each of the 10 Essential Skills and their accompanying concepts and theories. The primary focus will be on their role in ministerial and Christian leadership; in both the ministry and marketplace. We'll also discuss how this book and accompanying series can impact your leadership journey for the better.

Leadership is one of the most exciting explorations a person can undertake. So I'm excited to partner with you on this journey. Get ready to dig in. Plan to take some good notes. Be determined to apply what you learn. And be quick to pass on what you learn. Application and sharing of what you learn is the quickest way to internalize and own fresh knowledge.

DON'T LOOK OUT ONLY FOR YOUR OWN INTERESTS, BUT TAKE AN INTEREST IN OTHERS, TOO.

PHILIPPIANS 2: 3-4
NEW LIVING TRANSLATION

I had a desire, a passion, to help myself, but to also help others become the best leader they could possibly be.

Throughout the 10 Essential series I'll be sharing information from academic rigor, but most importantly from experience itself, as I attempt to use it and make sense of it in my own life and ministry.

DISCOURSE COMMUNITIES

The information we discuss in these pages I found by stumbling upon various **discourse communities**. These communities, found mostly in books and articles, were like entering a room where a conversation was already in progress. A particular discourse community is like attending a class in a foreign country where you first have to learn the language in order to understand.

> **DISCOURSE COMMUNITY**
> A group of people communicating with one another about common goals and interests.

Wisdom and due consideration dictate that when you enter such a room or community, you should first and foremost, listen—listen a lot. For each of us, active participation in the discourse community requires detailed attention to the talk that preceded entry into the room. So, do your best to learn as much as possible about the context of the conversation and what has been said prior to your entering. At some point you engage, join the dialogue, and become part of the conversation. Then you leave, knowing that the conversation continues without you.

Here at the outset, I want to set forth **the presuppositions and principles that undergird our discourse community and the 10 Essential Skills of leadership**.

THE LEADERSHIP LANDSCAPE

"The Lord will let the people be governed by immature boys. Everyone will take advantage of everyone else."

Isaiah 3:4-5 TEV

This passage found in Isaiah is thousands of years old, yet it seems so fresh and speaks so clearly to us today. Too often, this passage of scripture describes our present reality. We're not being led by people of character, not people of competence, but **IMMATURE BOYS**.

Then we hear, *"everyone will take advantage of everyone else"* i.e., climbing the ladder of success, getting to the top, and unconcerned about who we step on or how we get there. Self-protection and self-promotion are too often the driving forces and motivators. A sad but good example of what the leadership landscape looks like today.

Allow me to use an **Aesop's Fable** to explain. The fables were written to provide insight, a warning, a lesson. The fable used here is a story about greed and impatience, and by implication, contentment, patience, and perseverance.

The fable describes a man who has a goose that lays golden eggs. Every day he gets a golden egg from the goose. But in his greed and impatience the idea came to him to get all the golden eggs at once by cutting the goose open. When the deed was done, not a single golden egg did he find, and his precious goose was dead. The man learns that in his greed, he destroyed his wealth. By killing the goose, he destroyed all the future golden eggs.

This story and principle can be applied to leadership development and Christian formation as well. We want so much to find some magic elixir, some pixie dust, or someone who can wave a magic wand over our head and make us instantaneously competent and effective leaders.

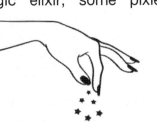

But it doesn't happen that way. There is no particular seminar, degree, course, book, video, or person you can talk to that can instantaneously make this happen to you. Because leadership development is not an event, it's a process.

Because leadership development is not an event, it's a process.

Personal development and Christian formation are like the goose that lays the golden egg. We cannot find or apply any one thing that will make us a competent and successful leader.

IT WILL TAKE A PROCESS.
It will take many things over time.

THE PROCESS OF PERSONAL DEVELOPMENT

So, in this series I'm going to expose you to theories, concepts, and ideas. It is my goal to equip you with a new vocabulary that will help you become the best individual and leader you can possibly be.

We don't want greed to take over our lives. We must develop patience. Stay away from any attempt to get it all at once, to get an immediate result. This one book is not going to do it. We will learn together to be life-long learners and life-long developers—_formation takes time._ The journey to being a better leader, a more effective leader; that process of growth and development is continual—it never ends.

LEADERLABS
FOUNDATIONAL PHILOSOPHY

1. THE CHURCH IS THE HOPE OF THE WORLD.
2. LEADERS ARE THE HOPE OF THE CHURCH.
3. THERE IS A LEADERSHIP CRISIS IN THE MARKETPLACE AND MINISTRY.
4. THE CRISIS IS A CRISIS OF CHARACTER AND COMPETENCE.

SECTION 2

FOUR
LEADERSHIP
DEVELOPMENT
PRESUPPOSITIONS

Our journey begins with what I refer to as our
leadership development presuppositions.
A presupposition is something assumed beforehand.
There are four presuppositions that undergird this program.

---

1 NUMBER ONE: A *Healthy* CHURCH IS THE *HOPE* OF THE WORLD.

For eleven years I served as Executive Director of People for Care and Learning (PCL). I spent a great deal of time in Southeast Asia, literally on the other side of the planet from the United States. During that season of my life, I was exposed to multiple leaders from scores of countries. I also came in contact with people living in desperate situations, deep poverty. I saw first-hand and up close just how important the church is in giving "hope" to the world.

GOD IS NOT CALLING US TO GO TO CHURCH; HE IS CALLING US TO BE HIS CHURCH, THE HOPE OF THE WORLD.

It does, however, need to be a *healthy* church, i.e., a church that understands its mission and purpose., a church that is led by a *healthy* pastor who understands the importance of "shared vision," a vison that encompasses both mission and maintenance mindsets and values. The church must be maintained. It must be responsible for its integrity, its responsibilities, and thus its credibility, so that it can be MISSIONAL.

As Christians, we walk in dynamic tension—being taught to "be *in* the world, but not *of* the world." Jesus prayed in John 17:15,

> "My prayer is not that you take them out of the world but that you protect them from the evil one."

The New Testament teaches that we are not to become *entangled* with the world. To this end, Paul wrote to the Ephesians,

> "You once walked *according to* **the course of this world,** according to the prince of the power of the air, the spirit who now works in the sons of disobedience ..."
>
> Ephesians 2:2

The words *"course of this world"* carries the meaning of current or flow. To be sure, there is an undertow, a subtle current that runs against and in contradiction to the will and the way of God. And yet, Jesus ate with publicans and sinners (Mark 2:16). Nearly everyone He associated with was an outcast. But His relationship with them was not purely social; **it was redemptive.**

Christians are, therefore, **like the gulf stream**, which is in the ocean and yet not part of it. This mysterious current defies the mighty Atlantic, ignores its tides, and flows steadily upon its course. Its color is different, being a deeper blue. Its temperature is different, being warmer. Its direction is different, being from south to north. It is in the ocean, and yet it is not part of it.

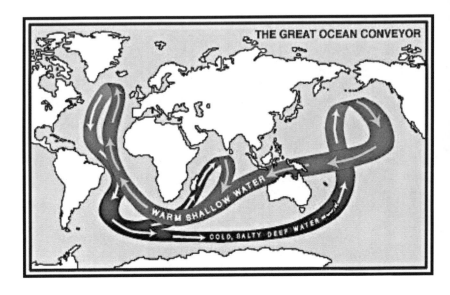

THE GULF STREAM

So, we as Christians are in the world. We come in contact with the world, and yet we are to retain our distinctive Christian character and refuse to let the world press us into its mold. It is our *distinctiveness* that lights the way. But this distinction is NOT to be dysfunction.

You don't have to go to a developing country to see people without hope. They're all around us, in every town, city, and community. They're our friends, family members, and colleagues, living in our neighborhoods.

The bible tells of a God who is on a mission. The incarnation is a story about that mission. A mission to redeem and to explain. To redeem humanity from the consequences of our own foolish choices and to explain to us who God is and what He is like.

John 1:14 and 18, says,

> "The Word became flesh and made his dwelling among us. We have seen his glory, the glory of the one and only Son, who came from the Father, full of grace and truth."

> "No one has ever seen God, but the one and only Son, who is himself God and is in closest relationship with the Father, has made him known."

The New English Bible reads, ***"Now the Word became flesh and took up residence among us."*** But I prefer the way the Message Bible says it,

> **"The Word became flesh and blood, and moved into the neighborhood."**

This passage of scripture was impressed upon me early during my missionary experience in Southeast Asia. How was I to reach a Buddhist-Hindu culture? *IF* the good news of Jesus' redemptive plan was my primary objective, then how was it to be accomplished when no one in Southeast Asia knew about the bible or Jesus? We were to **"move into the neighborhood."** We were to allow that culture to see our *good works* and, therefore, Jesus, through our lives and ministry—through our good works.

> "Let your good deeds shine out for all to see, so that everyone will praise your heavenly Father."

> Matthew 5:16

Every local church and mission around the world have the same mandate, the same mission and purpose—seek and save that which is lost (Luke 19:10), and minister to the poor and needy (Matthew 25:36). Care for them. Give them hope. For when you have done this unto the least of these, you have done it unto Jesus (Matthew 25:40).

God is looking for leaders "after his own heart." Leaders who submit to leading through service and trust him for the outcomes. A leader's character, therefore, matters because God is calling us to join Him in changing the world.

LEADERSHIP AND THE KINGDOM

The coming of the Kingdom of God is not just about some heavenly future; it is very much intended to play out right here on earth. We are invited and directed to participate in his great redemptive rescue mission.

We can thus conclude that the central message and mission of Jesus' incarnation was to purposefully inaugurate and establish God's Kingdom on earth. In fact, it seemed that Jesus was preoccupied with the coming of the Kingdom, mentioning it more than 100 times.

> "Thy Kingdom come, thy will be done, on earth as it is in heaven."
>
> Matthew 6:20

We are encouraged to join the Kingdom revolution by repudiating the values of this world; greed, arrogance, selfishness, hatred, racism, sexism, domination, exploitation, corruption. We are, conversely, to MODEL the values of the Kingdom: love, forgiveness, justice, integrity, compassion, sacrifice, encouragement, generosity, humility, and inclusion.

New Testament scholar, Pauline theologian, and Anglian Bishop, N. T. Wright, wrote,

> "Our task as image-bearing, God-loving, Christ-shaped, Spirit-filled Christians, following Christ and shaping our world, is to announce redemption to a world that has discovered its BROKENESS, to proclaim love and trust to a world that knows only exploitation, fear and suspicion....the gospel of Jesus points us and indeed urges us to be at the leading edge of the whole culture, articulating in STORY, and music and art and philosophy and education and poetry and politics and theology and even—heaven help us—biblical studies, a worldview that will mount the historically-rooted Christian challenge to both modernity and postmodernity, leading the way...with joy and humor and gentleness and good judgment and true wisdom."
>
> We must face the question, "if not now, then when?" If we are grasped by this vision, we may also hear the question, "if not us, then who?" And if the gospel of Jesus is not THE KEY to this task, then what is?"'

2 NUMBER TWO: *HEALTHY* LEADERS ARE THE HOPE OF THE CHURCH

If you're reading this book, you're looking to sharpen your saw and become the best leader you can be. You are either a leader now, trying to get out of the deep end of the pool, or you are an emerging leader and will be in leadership in the near future. In fact, I believe that everyone can be and is a leader. We just need to be more aware of it and more intentional about it.

You might be a staff or team member, a key volunteer, a pastor, state-level leader, someone in the ministry or marketplace, faith-based or business leader. **The KEY is to be a *HEALTHY* LEADER.** It is HEALTHY leaders that represent the hope of the church.

Years ago, I was in a hot, dirty van, driving down a dusty road in Cambodia near the Tonle Sap Lake, just outside the tourist destination town of Siem Reap.

I had just been appointed Executive Director of People for Care and Learning (PCL), an innovative Non-Government Organization (NGO) Nonprofit established by the Church of God World Missions Department to minister to the Buddhist-Hindu countries within Southeast Asia—Cambodia, Vietnam, Thailand, Laos, Burma, and Sri Lanka.

I was struggling to understand how I was to reach these people—what would ministry there look like? Suddenly it seemed that time stood still. As I looked into the eyes of an elderly Cambodian widow, these words were dropped into my spirit:

"INSPIRE HOPE, EMPOWER POTENTIAL."

These words became the architecture I would build ten years of ministry in Southeast Asia upon. In fact, these words became the fundamental structure I would also build LeaderLabs on. To this day, these words inspire, challenge and guide my life and ministry.

HOPE. HOPE is an interesting concept.

First, it is a component of **FAITH**. **Hebrews 11:1** says,

"Faith is the substance of things hoped for..."

Hope is an awakening of the human soul saying that life can be better than it is. Hope, therefore, is the soil from which potential grows. This *IS* the gospel...the GOOD NEWS!

Hope is the soil from which
potential grows.

These four words, "inspire hope, empower potential," along with John 1:14 (MG), became my north star—my guiding principle for ministry. Move into the neighborhood. Minister to the poor and needy. Let them see Jesus through your good works, and when you have to, use words to "inspire hope, and empower potential."

Earl Nightingale, a famous radio speaker and author (1921-1989) known for his syndicated five-minute radio commentary program, said,

> *"There exists in each of us great reservoirs of ability—even genius, that we habitually fail to use. It takes knowledge, care and time to bring that ability to the surface."*

Life, as it turns out, seems to, at its very nature, work at challenging our every desire to become the best version of ourselves. Our human condition since the fall of man, has been, and continues to be, a war between the flesh and the spirit.

As **A. W. Tozer** so truthfully explained in 1955, **"the bias of nature is always toward the wilderness, never toward the fruitful field."**

Paul articulated this in Romans 7, by saying,

> **"In practice, my own behavior baffles me. For I find myself not doing what I really want to do and doing what I really hate. So, if I do things I really don't want to do, it must be sin that has made its home in my nature"**
>
> (J. B. Phillips).

Then there is this thing called **POTENTIAL**.

Preacher, evangelist, and prolific writer, **G. Campbell Morgan,** wrote,

> **"We are all implanted with a seed of potential at the new birth."**

I refer to this as **"potential on steroids."** Potential is that which can be, but has not yet come into being; that which is actually possible but unrealized; that which is latent, invisible and inactive, lying hidden and undeveloped in a person.

Potential is something we all have, but not everyone realizes it to its fullest. In fact, it has sadly been said, "there is nothing more common than unsuccessful people with talent—with potential." This is why Ephesians 1:18 explains that we need to

> **"Have the eyes of our hearts enlightened, so that we may know what is the *HOPE* to which He has called us" (ESV).**

So, my life experience and God's calling has challenged me to work diligently to pull as many people as possible out of the land of broken unrealized dreams to realize their potential.

Professor of Psychology, Barbara Fredrickson, maintains that hope blossoms when crisis emerges, opening us to new creative possibilities. Hopeful people are "like the little engine that could, because they keep telling themselves **"I think I can, I think I can."**

There is, on one hand, what is called a naive "false hope;" positive thinking based on an unrealistic sense of optimism. Then there is **hope that is linked to the existence of A GOAL, combined with a determined plan for reaching that goal**.

The difference between hope and simple optimism is that real hope includes practical ways toward an improved future. This "I think I can" mentality involves the all-important **personal agency** – the belief that you can jump-start change and achieve your goals.

There is a tipping point, therefore, where despair turns into hope. Thus, our job as leaders is to create environments where people can see the actual possibilities of a better future—the *conviction* that tomorrow DOES NOT have to be like today.

We all need to hear again and again the words coming from Jeremiah 29:11-12,

> "For I know the plans I have for you," declares the Lord, "plans to prosper you and not to harm you, plans to give you **HOPE** and a future."

Truth is, who you are now, IS NOT who you CAN BE. This IS the GOSPEL. This is THE GOOD NEWS.

GOOD NEWS

3
NUMBER THREE:
THERE IS A LEADERSHIP CRISIS IN THE MARKETPLACE AND MINISTRY

Today's minister is called upon to be the shepherd of a flock and to lead an organization. But we see it every day in the news. There is a crisis of leadership both in the corporate world and in the church world. A recent headline said, "We need leaders, but we will accept much less." How sad.

"We need leaders, but we will accept much less."
newspaper headline

Leadership scandals have caused and continue to cause an erosion of confidence and a tremendous loss of faith in leadership around the world.

Dale Carnegie's findings make it especially disturbing, revealing studies from 2020 that suggest that leaders' performance in many organizations still have a long way to go:

- Just 15% of employees strongly agree that the leadership in their company makes them enthusiastic about the future.

- In another study, only 23% say that their leaders, overall, are effective.

So, **leadership makes a difference.**

Organizations, including the church, are facing two major challenges; one, finding and, two, developing leaders. They need to identify qualified candidates to fill current and future leadership roles. And they need to create a comprehensive leadership program—a leadership engine or pipeline to cultivate and develop the leaders of tomorrow.

EMPLOYEE ENGAGEMENT

A hot topic within the human resource departments of organizations is "employee engagement." But few people in ministry even know about the concept or just how important leadership is to this thing called *engagement*.

When employees, staff or key volunteers are "engaged," you get positive and quality results along with good morale. When they're not engaged you get alienation, low productivity, low quality, and poor customer service or dysfunctional relationships.

The term **"employee engagement"** describes a psychological commitment to one's work, team and organization. It's a mental state that fluctuates all the time, influenced by workplace relationships and events. Engaged employees are mentally *in the zone*, ready for action.

IN THE ZONE

Engaged employees are the engine that moves the organization forward on every level.

Engagement is the level of energy people bring to work or to the ministry—the level of enthusiasm they bring every time they show up. It's the difference between someone who just shows up to get paid and someone showing up and being enthusiastic about the work or ministry they do.

According to Gallup's *State of the Global Workplace: 2022 Report*, employees *who are not engaged* or *who are actively disengaged* cost the world $7.8 trillion in lost productivity.

Leaders are, therefore, now responsible for creating new work environments that are more resilient and adaptable to global shocks and organizational crises. My research supports these findings, revealing the competencies of resilience and adaptability to be in the top tier of needs for ministers as well.

WE ARE MAKING PROGRESS

We've come a long way during the past 150 years in terms of the way we treat employees, staff, teams and people who work for us and with us. In the past, organizations operated on what was known as **"Fordism,"** an assembly line mentality where people were seen as parts in a big machine.

Within Fordism, the only interest in people was that they perform their task quicker and more efficient. Things, for the most part, have changed for the better. The field of human resource management has grown and today we care about employees and treat them similar to the way we treat customers. Just like you want to have a customer that is satisfied, we want to have employees and church members who are also satisfied and more engaged. Some people have a problem seeing church members and people in our communities as customers. I kind of like the idea though. It causes us to think more in terms of service. As Christian leaders, we are to serve.

Research, however, shows that even with the progress, the average employee only brings approximately **30%** of their potential to work with them and this is *the amount of productivity a pay check produces.* So, if we are going to tap into that other 70%, we'll have to address other motivating factors.

Let's take a look at how this breaks down.

Consider first that only 29% of employees are **ENGAGED**, meaning they are loyal and psychologically committed to their job or role in ministry. These people are productive, work with passion and very connected to the organization. They also have a tendency to stay longer.

On the other hand, another 52%, are **NOT ENGAGED**. These people are sleepwalking through their days; checked out. They are putting time in, but no passion or energy. They are also more likely to leave.

The remaining 19% are **ACTIVELY DISENGAGED**. They are physically present but are busy acting out their unhappiness and undermining all other engagement. They are psychologically absent, unhappy and insist on sharing their unhappiness with others.

DOES LEADERSHIP MATTER?

The previously stated data tells us that most of the currently employed workforce, from all sectors, are **NOT ENGAGED.** And, should they leave their present position, they will most likely land again on less than engaged territory—a self-defeating and frustrating cycle.

But **the most effective interrupter of this dysfunctional cycle is the leader.** Consider Gallup's finding citing that *it takes more than a 20% pay raise to lure most employees away from a good leader or supervisor, one who engages them.* But it takes <u>next to nothing to steal most disengaged workers</u>.

Hogan Assessment Systems, a leadership development industry serving over half the Fortune 500, says there are a number of elements that determine engagement and represent the basic needs employees have when they come to work. Here's the top five:

1. They want a **BASIC JOB DESCRIPTION**—what's expected of them and what a good job looks like.

2. They want **OPPORTUNITIES TO LEARN and GROW**.

3. They are looking for a sense of **ACHIEVEMENT**—they want to have their accomplishments recognized and rewarded.

4. They are seeking a sense of **CAMARADERIE**. We are all social beings, wanting to work in collaboration and cooperation with others—usually in teams.

5. They are also seeking **EQUITY**. They want to be treated fairly, with dignity, as an adult human being.

When these five needs are met, people tend to be much more highly engaged.

Once again, Hogan Assessment Systems, the international leader in personality insights, says that *the primary factor cited for employee disengagement is an employee's boss* or supervisor; the leader.

People don't leave organizations. They leave people.

Typically, *disengagement* involves a boss who displays a lot of emotional outbursts and thus, their employees and teams, spend a lot of time and energy trying to avoid those outbursts by walking on egg shells.

ADVICE?

Become self-aware and make targeted behavioral changes to keep your emotions under control. Through this intervention a person can change their reputation.

It's true. **Unlocking your potential begins with knowing yourself.** And becoming aware of how you show up to others, how others perceive your behavior, is crucial to leadership effectiveness.

Behavior, unlike personality, can be changed. Behavior can be dialed up or dialed back. In fact, I've worked for years, using *behavioral* assessments to coach and help ministry leaders do just this—become aware of their behavioral tendencies, how they show up to others, and how to adjust when necessary—adapt. This simple process that first and foremost involves self-awareness, is transformational.

Proverbs 20:5 provides a perfectly descriptive metaphor: The reasons for your behavior, motivation, and intentions are like water in a deep well, but a person who seeks insight can draw them out.

We now know that certain behavioral characteristics attract engaged followers and certain behavioral characteristics create disengaged cultures. So, if organizations and ministries want productive, loyal, and engaged members, teams and employees, they need to **adopt two standard approaches**:

1. Hire people who fit benchmarked profiles.
2. Do targeted, individualized, assessment and training to help people become aware of their behavior and when necessary, dial it up and dial it back, thus changing their behavior or adapting.

Studying how a leader behaves is a critical part of understanding what drives engagement. And most of us have witnessed up close and personal, bad behavior from a leader at one time or another. The saddest result of such leadership is that the effects of a leader's behavior trickle down into the organization, which means, how a leader leads effects how healthy and effective the team is and how healthy the organizational culture and climate is.

THE WELL-BEING OF OUR PEOPLE

There are also people issues that do not usually show up on a spreadsheet—like employee/staff well-being. It is the responsibility of people-centered *superleaders* to pay attention to their people. If leaders are not paying attention to their team's well-being, they're likely to be blindsided by poor productivity, high quit rates and burnout. We're all too familiar now with terms like "the great resignation," and "the great discontent," as people quit their jobs at record levels.

"The Great Resignation is really the Great Discontent and the Great Reshuffle."

A **Gallup analysis** in 2021-2022, following the Covid-19 Pandemic, referred to this phenomenon as "the great reshuffle." They found that 48% of America's working population was actively job searching or watching for opportunities—with organizations facing a staggeringly high quit rate. Ministries experience the same issues.

 Gallup's *State of the Global Workplace* report (2022), the emotional side of work has not healed from the pressures that came with 2020 and the COVID-19 pandemic.

A **Harvard Business Review** (HBR) article reports that negative emotions are at a new high. And as of 2021 stress, worry, anger, and sadness had increased and remained above pre-pandemic levels. As of March 2022, a **Gallup Survey** found that fewer than 1 in 4 U.S. employees felt that their employer cared about their well-being.

Employee, staff, and team-care starts in the CEO's office. The same is true for the church and denomination at all levels of leadership.

HBR says that of all the lessons learned from the pandemic of 2020, this one should be near the top of the list: **Employee well-being is crucial to organizational health.** Organizations can't function effectively — let alone, adapt, compete, survive — with struggling, suffering, sad, disengaged and often angry employees and/or staff members.

Employee well-being is a risk and an opportunity that leaders can't afford to ignore. These are pastoral issues for sure, but all Christian leaders, in every field, must take responsibility for people-care.

 Employee well-being is crucial to organizational health.

MANAGEMENT VERSUS LEADERSHIP

Another growing awareness involves the fact that **there are fundamental differences between a manager and a leader**.

Leaders influence, inspire and drive people toward a common goal. But the role of a manager is to keep the day-to-day operations of an organization running smoothly.

Development programs must reflect these differences. **Leaders have people follow them while managers have people work for them**. Both are essential.

Problem is, **we now have too many managers and not enough LEADERS**. Development Dimensions International's (DDI) research from 2020 revealed **a leadership shortage on a global scale**. There are plenty of managers. But leaders are in short supply. The far-reaching implications of this fact cannot be underestimated.

LEADERS
INFLUENCE, INSPIRE AND DRIVE PEOPLE TOWARD A COMMON GOAL.

MANAGERS
KEEP THE DAY-TO-DAY OPERATIONS OF AN ORGANIZATION RUNNING SMOOTHLY.

TOO MANY MANAGERS NOT ENOUGH LEADERS

Leadership is essential for adaptation and change, and change is hitting us like a tsunami. Change has changed and if we're not careful, we will run into something before we even see it.

We need leaders.

Consider the following statistics:

- **4 OUT OF 10 NEW HIRES WILL FAIL WITHIN THEIR FIRST 18 MONTHS.**

- **4 OUT OF 10 CEO'S WILL FAIL WITHIN THEIR FIRST 12 MONTHS.**

- **ONLY 1 IN 10 EMPLOYEES GET PROMOTED EACH YEAR.**

WHY?

In one way or another, people fail to grow. They fail to learn. Personal growth and development are not something nice to have, but ESSENTIAL to your calling and ministerial career.

Learning and the consequential growth of a leader is like oxygen to a deep-sea diver—without it you will die.

When you stop growing, your influence erodes. Over time you lose the opportunity to lead anyone at all. If you want to lead, you must grow. Research estimates that leadership is about 1/3 natural talent and 2/3 developed. That is great news!

4 NUMBER FOUR: THE LEADERSHIP CRISIS IS A CRISIS OF CHARACTER, COMPETENCE, AND CREDIBILITY

We not only need to be men and women of character, but we also need to know what we're doing. Not only what we're doing, but how to do it with excellence. There's nothing worse than trying to follow someone or have someone who's directly over you that really "doesn't know their stuff." So, we want to be people of character and competence. It's not a question of either-or. We desperately need both.

Our credibility is built on the foundation of our character and competence. Credibility is believability. We want to be people of…

**INTEGRITY
CREDIBILITY
COMPETENCY**

When we boil it all down, we want leaders who are…

HONEST.

According to **Kouzes and Posner**, in their book, *"The Leadership Challenge,"* when followers are asked,

> *"What is the number one characteristic that you want in leaders who you would willingly follow?"*

It boils down to **honesty**; top of the list.

If we are not people of integrity, people who are honest, then those around us will not trust us or believe us. And **if** *THEY* **don't believe us, the MESSENGERS, then they will not believe our MESSAGE**.

FIRST LAW OF LEADERSHIP

"If we don't believe in the messenger, we won't believe the message."

James Kouzes and Barry Z. Posner

Bottom line: Without character there is no **TRUST**. Without trust there are no **FOLLOWERS**, and without followers, **LEADERSHIP** does not exist.

We often assume that leadership begins with CHARACTER, but in reality, *the opportunity to lead often begins with technical competence.*

- The best player on the team
- The high achiever
- The most articulate
- The best preacher
- The best teacher
- The smartest
- The strongest
- The most attractive

In most circumstances, people with these characteristics are the ones tapped for leadership. So, competence is extremely important to leadership emergence.

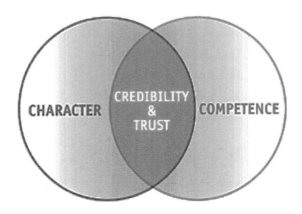

We do, however, need to qualify the character-competence balance. The *essential competency* I speak of is referred to as **"threshold competency,"** — a demonstrable competency concerning the basic roles and responsibilities of a specific job or ministry position within a certain context or demographic.

For example: Today, a ministry leader needs skill as a good communicator and preacher; but, during *this new season*, he or she must also be competent at meeting budgets, deadlines, and administrating a team. These skills require a leader to *perform at some level of expectation as well.* Without these additional skills, a ministry leader will often find themselves with NO CREDIBILITY for leadership and very little change in his/her pocket when it comes to leading change and adaptation.

So, it's true; character is the root and competence is the fruit.

Proverbs 27:9
"As water reflects a face, so a man's heart reflects the man."

In terms of character, who you are on the inside, your heart, really reflects the person you are. So, we want to give ourselves first and foremost to the development of character.

THE IMPORTANCE OF LEADERS WITH CHARACTER

The late Bill Bright, director of Campus Crusade for Christ, said, *"One billion new Christians will be born worldwide into the Kingdom and the church will need five million new leaders."*

"One billion new Christians will be born worldwide into the Kingdom and the church will need five million new leaders."

I want you to join the army, this incredible community of Christian leaders in both the marketplace and ministry, who are striving to be the best they can be so that we can do what we need to do in this incredibly exciting time we find ourselves living in today.

SHARPEN THE SAW

Proverbs 24:30-31 speaks to us about being disciplined in our approach to learning.

> **"I went by the field of the slothful, and by the vineyard of the man void of understanding; And lo, it was all grown over with thorns, and nettles had covered the face thereof, and the stone wall thereof was broken down."**

The writer is talking to the slothful, lazy people who show no interest, people who show no enthusiasm, no concern, but do things half-heartedly.

Being educated and being a person who seeks knowledge does not tell me everything about you, but when you seek as much knowledge as you can, it tells me you're not a person who cuts corners. You're not a person looking for the path of least resistance. You're a person willing to pay the price to be the best you that you can be. It tells me that you're a person of positive and righteous influence. You're a person of ambition, determination and personal pride.

So, if you're a seeker of knowledge, congratulations. Welcome to the incredible army that understands that being an effective leader is a process and it's fundamentally about personal development.

Personal development and becoming the best version of yourself is about making a commitment to being a life-long learner and creating learning organizations.

The Apostle Paul speaks to our role in this process in Ephesians 4:1-2 (KJV),

"I beseech you to walk worthy of your calling."

In the New Living Translation Paul "begs" us to *lead a life* worthy of our calling. I like that. **LEAD A LIFE**.

Look at the implication of what Paul is saying here. Whose life can you lead any better than your own? This may be common sense, but as Ken Blanchard says, *"common sense is not always common practice."*

"Common sense is not always common practice."
Ken Blanchard

We try to help others lead their lives, but our own life is not being led. We're not ordering our own private world. So, over and over in scripture we hear that we are to take care of ourselves first.

Question

Why would anyone want to be **led** by you?

Let's change it up and now talk about the *four* undergirding leadership development *principles* for the 10 Essential Skills.

10 ESSENTIAL SKILLS
FOUNDATIONAL
PRINCIPLES

1) Leadership Development begins with Self-Development.

2) Self-Development begins with Self-Awareness.

3) Self-Awareness leads to Self-Control or Self-Management.

4) Self-Management leads to Character, Competence, and Credibililty.

SECTION 3

FOUR
LEADERSHIP
DEVELOPMENT
PRINCIPLES

① LEADERSHIP DEVELOPMENT BEGINS WITH SELF-DEVELOPMENT

In the first chapter of James, the brother of Jesus tells us that the word of God, the bible, is literally like **A MIRROR**. When we look into the pages of the bible, we don't see others first, we see ourselves.

"Anyone who listens to the word but does not do what it says is like someone who looks at his face in a mirror 24 and, after looking at himself, goes away and immediately forgets what he looks like. 25 But whoever looks intently into the perfect law that gives freedom, and continues in it—not forgetting what they have heard, but doing it— they will be blessed in what they do."

James 1:23-25 (NIV)

This passage is emphasizing this underpinning and foundational principle of self-development. And that leadership development, counterintuitively, begins with **SELF-DEVELOPMENT**.

Steven Covey, in his book, *The Seven Habits of Highly Effective People,* describes Habit Two as "Beginning with the end in mind." We need to use this principle, this habit, here. Self-development is often overlooked, especially within Christian circles, because it seems to be a selfish act. But, in fact, we have to begin here because **you cannot help anyone if your own life is a mess.**

You cannot help anyone if your own life is a mess.

But it's our destination—the end goal—that justifies this foundational principle.

Peter Senge, a systems scientist, and senior lecturer at MIT Sloan School of Management, provides a wonderful explanation of this paradoxical attitude—one, that as we'll see during our continued development journey, is also very biblical.

Peter Senge's definition of leadership states:

"Leadership is
(1) the capacity of a
human community
(2) to shape
and influence its future."

Senge's first thought within his definition addresses a fundamental trap that we often fall into when thinking about leaders and leadership. The **hero-great man trap**—that it's all about the individual. And while the development of a leader starts with self-development, it is definitely *NOT* about the individual. It's an oxymoron.

OXYMORON
A figure of speech in which apparently contradictory
terms appear in conjunction.
A word of phrase that contradicts itself.

When we step back and examine the product, the end result and outcome of leadership, what actually gets accomplished—it happens through a **COLLECTIVE**.

While personal growth and development, an individual's capacities, are very important, the **OUTCOMES** are inherently collective.

The second part of Senge's definition involves what he refers to as **FUTURE CREATIVE ORIENTATION**. Orientation is fundamental to leadership—how we shape our future, how we bring it into being, things we really care about, how we accomplish things that really matter.

Senge is referring to leadership that cast a vision so powerful and captivating that people sign up for the long march and commit to making that vision become a reality.

But this can't happen without **SELF-DEVELOPMENT.**

I entered into the ministry more than four decades ago, and when I started out, I read books, listened to sermons and teachings, mostly with other people in mind; saying to myself, *"This is good preaching material. This will really help THEM."*

But I've since learned that we have to listen for ourselves, too; train ourselves and create mental models that cause us to think and behave differently. It is true, leadership development and Christian formation begins with self-development; we have to begin by working on ourself FIRST.

We have to begin by working on ourself FIRST.

In fact, greater insight to yourself will help you to have greater insight to other people. Therefore, making you a better leader.

It has been said that the first job and responsibility of leadership is to somehow get the best out of OTHERS. But we need to turn this on its head and say it this way; the first job of leadership is getting the best out of yourself.

The first job of leadership is getting the best out of yourself.

As you get the best out of yourself, you'll become equipped to get the best out of others – helping them to become the best versions of themselves, too.

Mark Sanborn, in his book, ***The Potential Principle***, says, "We all know how good we are right now—but we don't know how good we could be."

Gordon Alport (1897-1967), an American psychologist, said, "The self in each of us is constantly striving to reach its maximum potential and knowledge of self is the biggest modifier of behavior there is."

> **"Knowledge of self is the biggest modifier of behavior there is."**

Research still agrees with Alport, telling us that almost all people have a desire to get better. In fact, as much as 68% say they have a *commitment* to get better, but only 30% actually have a plan. Without a plan, that is simply wishful thinking.

FEAR is not an *option*.
LUCK is not a *strategy*.
HOPE is not a *plan*.

For example, researchers in Great Britain worked with 248 people to help them build better exercise habits. They divided them into three groups, a control group, a motivation group, and a group with a plan.

The control group was asked to only track how often they exercised. This group improved by **35%**. The motivation group was given a motivation speech, asked to keep a record of their exercise, and to read about the benefits of exercise. This group improved by **38%**.

The third group, the group with a plan, was also given the motivation speech—to do all the above *and* to formulate a plan as to when and where they would exercise. Specifically, each member of the third group completed the following **commitment sentence**:  "During the next week, I will partake in at least 20 minutes of vigorous exercise on [DAY] at [TIME] in [PLACE]." This group improved by **91%**.

The sentence the third group filled out is what researchers refer to as an ***implementation intention***, which is a plan you make beforehand about when and where to act. That is, how you intend to implement a particular habit.

If this (Cue Situation).
Then that (Behavioral Response)

The cues that can trigger a habit, both good and bad, are diverse—but the two most common cues are **time and location**.

An Implementation intention leverages both of these cues. An implementation intention sweeps away foggy notions and transforms your intention into concrete plans of action.

Many people think they lack MOTIVATION. What they really lack is CLARITY.

Peter Drucker (1909-2005), the father of modern management, added further insight by explaining, "We spend a lot of time teaching leaders what to do. We don't spend enough time teaching leaders *what to stop*." "Half the leaders I've met," said Drucker, "don't' need to learn what to do. They need to **learn** *what to stop*." So, *FOCUS, is the ability to find the big "YES" and saying "no" a thousand times.*

It is SELF-KNOWLEDGE *plus* the APPLICATION of that knowledge that equals EFFECTIVENESS.

Self-Knowledge + Application = EFFECTIVENESS

So, in this book and in this series, I want you to get all the knowledge you possibly can. I want you to ask the right questions as to how to apply this information and be intentional about it.

It seems, then, that <u>intentionality needs a partner</u>.

Changing behavior is all about being deliberate and purposeful. So, I believe **THE MOST IMPORTANT** variable for changing behavior is <u>**TENACITY**</u> — persistence, determination—what the bible calls "**PERSEVERANCE.**" You have to have **RESOLVE**.

 Think about it, **"What if you were given the choice, change or die?"** Make tough decisions about the way you think and behave, or your time will end soon.

Could you change?

Fast Company magazine cited scientifically studied odds saying the deck is stacked against you—**9 to 1**—against you. Wow!

$$\frac{9}{1}$$

Consider this. Health care in the USA is a $1.8 Trillion a year problem. Primarily due to diseases that are very well known and fundamentally behavioral. In other words, most of these people are sick because of how they choose to live their lives.

In fact, 80% of the United States' healthcare budget is consumed on **5 behavioral issues**:

1. Smoking
2. Drinking
3. Eating
4. Stress
5. Not enough exercise.

80%

There are 1.3 million heart patients per year costing $30 billion, many of which could avoid relapses by switching to a healthier lifestyle—yet few do. Two years after their surgery, 90% have not changed their lifestyle.

Changing the behavior of people is the biggest challenge of healthcare. According to **John Kotter** at Harvard University, changing the behavior of people is also the biggest challenge in businesses and ministries.

It turns out that CEO's, the leaders of all organizations, are the prime change agents for their company, church or non-profit. But they're often as resistant to change as anyone else—and just as prone to backsliding once the change initiative has started.

You would think that a crisis would be a powerful motivator for personal or organizational change. But severe heart disease is among the most serious of personal crises, and it doesn't motivate—at least not nearly enough.

So, what are we to do?

Behavior change happens most often when we speak to people's emotions. We must include all the facts.  Give them the right information, but **we must go beyond the facts and consider the psychological, emotional, and spiritual.** We must consider a "holistic approach."

We must learn to recast the reasons for change. Motivating people out of *fear* simply does not work all the time. So, reframe the issue. Inspire them with a new vision of "the joy of living," Cast a shared vision that reveals a future so desirable that they can't wait to sign up for the long-march. It turns out that **joy is a more powerful motivator than fear.**

And do not underestimate the value of short-term wins. Without sufficient wins that are visible, timely, unambiguous and meaningful to others, change efforts invariably run into serious problems.

90% of heart patients could not change their behavior. But **77% of another group did change their behavior.** How? They held weekly support groups.

You can't do it alone.

UNDERSTANDING THE PLATEAU
OF LATENT POTENTIAL

Author **James Clear**, in his best-selling book, *"Atomic Habits,"* explains the truth about the *Plateau of Latent Potential and the valley of disappointment*. It represents **the lag time between what you think should happen and what actually happens**. In other words, progress doesn't happen in a linear fashion because the results of your efforts are often delayed. It isn't until months or years later that you realize the value of the previous work you have done.

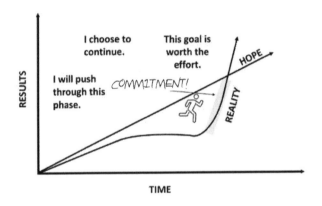

Too many people give up too soon. It's frustrating when you don't get the results you were expecting. We want the quick fix, the immediate result, the microwave version of what only comes through a process that requires discipline and time—what was referred to previously as **RESOLVE**.

We see the success of others, or how they have changed, and we assume they experienced what amounted to an overnight success. We assume they started at a certain point and moment by moment witnessed the transformation they had as their goal. There simply is, however, no achievement without first experiencing the journey across the plateau of latent potential and through the valley of disappointment.

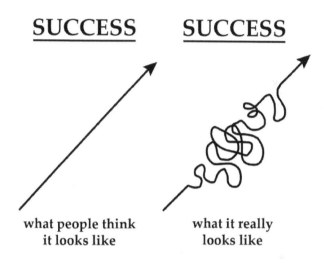

SUCCESS   SUCCESS

what people think   **what it really**
it looks like   **looks like**

We think that we should see results immediately, but in reality, it's like planting seed. It takes time to see results. **Potential** is real, but it's lying dormant. Potential represents *the capacity* to become or develop into something in the future. It's not realized yet. And sadly, potential is often used in a negative sense, to describe someone who possessed it, but never realized it. We say, "they *HAD* such great potential."

RESULTS, too, brought about by hard work and disciplined effort, can also be realized, but sustained and intentional behavior is required over time—you must break through that plateau of latent potential. An ice cube will not begin to melt until the temperature reaches 33 degrees. Water will not boil until it reaches the temperature of 212 degrees.

BREAKTHROUGH MOMENT

There is that **"breakthrough moment"** that is the result of many previous actions that build up the potential required to unleash major change. Up until that breakthrough moment, your work, your effort, is not being wasted, it is just being stored.

It is again, what **James Clear** refers to as, *"The Power of the Plus One,"* the power of tiny, consistent gains. Will I choose to become 1% better each day, or 1% worse each day?

Basic truth about Leadership:

Everything looks like and feels like a failure in the middle. You cannot give up when you hit the first obstacle to your dream or goal. You must PERSIST, PERSEVERE, KEEP MOVING; LEARNING, REDIRECTING, CELEBRATING small victories.

SITUATIONAL LEADERSHIP

Addressing the #1 Mistake Leaders Make – Attempting to Lead Everyone the Same Way

This same principle is taught in **Ken Blanchard's** Situational Leadership model. The model reveals four styles of leadership that should match four accompanying developmental levels of a follower.

STYLE 1: DIRECT   **D1:** Enthusiastic Beginner
STYLE 2: COACH   **D2:** Disillusioned Learner
STYLE 3: SUPPORT   **D3:** Capable, but Cautious
STYLE 4: DELEGATE   **D4:** Self-reliant Achiever

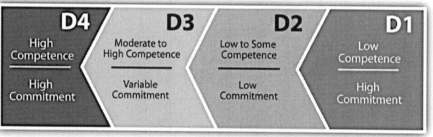

D4	D3	D2	D1
High Competence	Moderate to High Competence	Low to Some Competence	Low Competence
High Commitment	Variable Commitment	Low Commitment	High Commitment

Developed ◄———————————————— Developing
Development Level of the Individual

Every follower starts the developmental and learning process for every goal or task at the D1 Developmental Level. The Enthusiastic Beginner is excited about the new opportunity and brings a great deal of energy to the table. Their need at this level is direction—they need to know what a good job looks like. Problem is—they don't know what they don't know and as time moves on, they fall into **Developmental Level #2, Disillusioned Learner**.

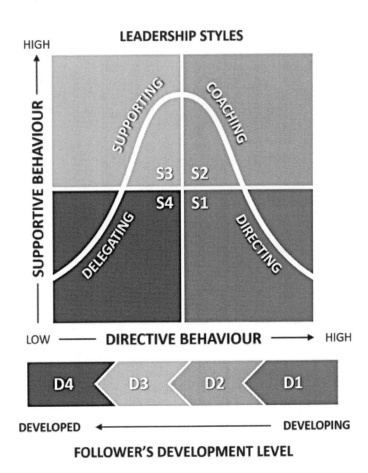

The Disillusioned Learner, all of a sudden, begins to see what they didn't see, and begins to understand that the goal or task is much more difficult than first realized. It will cost them more and require more effort. There's a bigger learning curve than expected. They become disillusioned. This is where so many people give up, drop out, quit, and walk away.

Truth is, however, it's only a phase within the developmental process. Once again, perseverance and resolve are needed, along with a good dose of tenacity, to push through to the next developmental level.

We can all think of times in our lives when we wanted to quit. It happens all the time. I remember when I was learning to ride a bike. I was so excited that Christmas morning, but I all too soon became disillusioned thinking to myself, "I'll never learn to ride a bike. This is way too hard." But I did learn to ride.

Pushing through the Disillusioned Level will bring you to **Developmental Level 3, Capable, but Cautious Performer**, and then on toward **Developmental Level 4, Self-Reliant Achiever**.

The Plateau of Latent Potential, Valley of Disappointment, and Disillusioned Learner stage of development are principles of leadership development, personal growth, and Christian formation that need to be understood, expected, and taught. Way too much potential has been lost to the ash heap of *"what could have been"* simply because we gave up HOPE.

The second foundational principle says "Self-Development begins with Self-Awareness.

2 SELF-DEVELOPMENT BEGINS WITH SELF-AWARENESS

Research focusing on leadership has not been able to find one *best model* of leadership, but we do know that an effective leader is one who leads an effective team. And if you want to be successful, you'd better understand yourself and your teammates.

Who you are determines how you lead. And how you lead determines how a group will function, which determines how an organization will function.

If being *perceived* as being right for a leadership role is the same as being right for a leadership role, then why do we have so many bad leaders? Perception does not always translate into someone who is capable for the job. So, the real challenge is learning about yourself and being determined to never stop learning.

Seventy-five members of the Stanford Graduate School of Business Advisory Council provided a recommendation as to **THE** most important capability for leaders to develop. It was...

SELF-AWARENESS.

And then again, common sense is not common practice. As elementary as it seems, **we must know enough about ourselves to lead others**.

SELF-AWARENESS IS *THE* ABSOLUTE, NUMBER ONE, FUNDAMENTAL, PREREQUISITE FOR PERSONAL GROWTH, DEVELOPMENT, AND CHRISTIAN FORMATION.

In fact, my task in this book and throughout the entire 10 Essential Skills series is to facilitate a learning experience that will guide you through a process of self-discovery and assist you in the development of **WISDOM**.

Self-Discovery

Wisdom is an incredibly important concept because wisdom has to do with a person's ability **to effectively use what they know**.

We don't think about this in learning situations very often. But the goal is to collect this intellectual information and knowledge, to hear something exhilarating, something novel, something new, possibly something you've heard before, but you hear it in a different way, and "put it into practice," to become a person with wisdom.

When we think about wisdom, we typically conger up an image of someone who is calm, cool, and collected in the midst of what is often tumultuous situations. They just remain calm.

Nowadays, it seems we are bombarded by crises and tough situations. In fact, Development Dimensions International (DDI), a global leadership development and human resources consulting firm, sites findings from their 2021 global research that says, **"we are entering a time defined as a season of continual crisis."**

"We are entering a time defined as a season of CONTINUAL CRISIS."
DDI INTERNATIONAL 2021 GLOBAL RESEARCH

This brings up the importance of understanding our **INNER ELEPHANT** and our **INNER CEO**. These are metaphors used to help us understand what's going on with the struggle inside each of us.

The inner elephant is huge, strong, powerful, often illogical and emotional, and it is prone to control us.

There is also the inner CEO, that if accessed and utilized, with intentionality and fervency, is able to take control of the inner elephant. The inner CEO is more logical, rational, and is able to take control – it's called **SELF-CONTROL**.

The Apostle Paul speaks to this issue and reveals the inner elephant in **Romans 7:25**,

> *"I do not understand my own actions. For I do not do what I want, but I do the very thing I hate. I can will what is right, but I cannot do it."*

Has it ever seemed to you like an essential part of you *"looked the other way"* while Dick Dastardly or Fiendish Fay, *some rogue aspect of you took over*? There are times when it seems—

- Our impulses kidnap us,
- Our thoughts mislead us,
- Our behaviors mystify us,
- Our emotions know no reason.

There are times when we unnecessarily complicate our own

lives. The bigger problem arises when given enough time & repetition (habit), **self-sabotaging hijacks** like these can become enduring patterns that go unnoticed until punctured by A MOMENT OF TRUTH.

We can see and understand clearly the struggle between the inner elephant and the inner CEO. We see scripture speaking to us with candor, transparency, and simplicity about the importance of **SELF-CONTROL** and the accompanying idea of **SELF-AWARENESS**.

Matthew 7:5 (NAS),

"First take the log out of *your own eye,*
**and then you will see clearly to take
the speck out of your brother's eye."**

Galatians 6:1 (NIV),
"But watch *yourself,*
or you also may be tempted."

Romans 12:3 (NIV),
"Think of yourself with sober judgment."

Galatians 6:4 (NAS),
"Let each one examine his own words."

Over and over, scripture brings us to this principle that tells us that **a few moments of brutal self-honesty is worth more than a lifetime of self-deception.**

A few moments of
brutal self-honesty
is worth more
than a lifetime
of self-deception.

Let me encourage you to open your heart and to be brutally honest with yourself throughout the reading of this book and throughout this entire 10 Essential Skills series.

Take a close look at YOURSELF. Because knowing your authentic self will require courage and honesty.

In fact, many people today attempt to establish themselves in the world of leadership but they leave very little time for **SELF-EXPLORATION**.

   **SELF-ASSESSMENT**

Here are a few questions to assist you in your journey of self-awareness.

- Are you an introvert or extrovert?
- Are you detailed oriented or socially-oriented?
- Do you like time moving fast or slow?
- Do you like to talk or listen?
- Do you prefer rules or being a pioneer?
- Are you a thinker or a feeler?
- Do you prefer working alone or with a team?
- Do you prefer function or form?

Every Leader Carries Two Buckets

It's one of the most fundamental leadership concepts. Every leader carries two buckets—a **TASK Bucket** and a **RELATIONSHIP Bucket**. We also have a propensity to pour out of one of these buckets more than the other. Which one more represents you?

The goal is *TO LEARN* to pour out of each bucket according to what each situation and/or follower needs.

Truly, self-development begins with self-awareness.

This brings us to our third foundational principle of this series.

SELF-AWARENESS LEADS TO SELF-CONTROL, SELF-MANAGEMENT & SELF-LEADERSHIP

The bible says in **Proverbs 25:28** (TLB),

"A man without self-control is as defenseless as a city with broken-down walls."

Your inner elephant is often a very poor leader. Your inner elephant needs direction from your inner CEO to overcome tendencies and propensities that we all have to overreact, be impulsive, procrastinate, give in to temptation, and have a lack of focus. We can overcome these things, but it will require persistence.

WHAT WE SEEM TO BE LEARNING ABOUT LEADERSHIP

During the past fifty years, leadership scholars have conducted thousands of studies trying to find definitive styles, characteristics, and personality traits of great leaders.

One thing stands out and is clear:

There is no clear profile of the IDEAL LEADER.

There is no cookie-cutter leadership style.

It is clear that there is much diversity in what we see as leadership. Therefore, we need to learn all we can about leadership because, this we do know—all leadership is context-sensitive.

All leadership is context-sensitive.

For instance, the leader's job, in this day and time, is no longer command and control. We're no longer, as a leader, standing on top of a pyramid barking down commands and directives to subordinates below us.

A leader's job today is to inspire and encourage, cultivate and coordinate the motivations and actions of other people.

All of which brings me to my two favorite words regarding leadership:

"IT DEPENDS"

Let me explain. There was a time when change was incremental, and change inherently, most of the time, provided time to pick and choose from a cookie-cutter slate of options and best practices. A leader could fundamentally pull an idea off the shelf, follow steps one, two, and three and experience the outcomes described in the instructions. The times, however, they have changed.

My two favorite words, "It Depends," come from what is called, **Contingency Theory.** Contingency theory is a behavioral theory based on the view that there is "no best way" to lead an organization, get something done, or make a decision. The theory states that all these actions are dependent, or contingent on many internal and external factors or variables. So, **leaders today, more than ever before, have to THINK.** We also have to use extreme wisdom when attempting to give advice.

Leadership involves a multitude of variables. It requires both wisdom and judgment. And wisdom and judgment come from the marriage of knowledge and experience.

The questions come and the answers are found in individual situations and contexts. Thus, IT DEPENDS.

For instance, within leadership scenarios there are few "if a, then b" solutions.

Rather, it is "if a, then b" when faced with today's circumstances. Tomorrow it very well could be "if *a*, then *c* or *d* or *e* or *f* or ...

PENTECOSTAL-WESLEYAN ROOTS

The things we've been discussing are not new ideas. **John Wesley,** the founder of Evangelical Methodism (1791) struggled with this issue, too.

ARE LEADERS BORN, OR ARE LEADERS MADE?

John Wesley, said, *"YES,"* and I agree.

Leaders are born and they are made.

Leaders have both **NATURAL GIFTS** and **ACQUIRED GIFTS** and Wesley used a principle from **Exodus 3:21-22** (BSB) that he referred to as

"Plundering the Egyptians."

> "And I will grant this people such favor in the sight of the Egyptians that when you leave, you will not go away empty-handed. Every woman shall ask her neighbor and any woman staying in her house for silver and gold jewelry and clothing, and you will put them on your sons and daughters.
> So, **you will plunder the Egyptians."**
>
> *See Heitzenrater, Pulpit and Pew, *"Take Thou Authority"*

We, therefore, not only use **SPECIAL REVELATION** that we find in scripture, but we also use truths we find in intellectual data or what we refer to as **GENERAL REVELATION**.

We, therefore, sift all information through the pages of scripture in order to help us sharpen the saw and be the best that we can be.

The bar was high with John Wesley. Wesley's criteria and expectations for ministers was above the reach of most people and definitely not easily achieved – it involved rigor.

JOHN WESLEY'S HIGH BAR:

Know Soteriology – the work of God (doctrine of salvation).
Know Biblical scholarship – the word of God (the Bible).
Know Greek and Hebrew – the biblical languages.
Know the early Church fathers – church history.
Know secular history – know it so we don't repeat it.
Know science – the act of good and logical thinking.
Know psychology and sociology – the constitution of man.
Know common sense – consideration of circumstances.
Know ministerial ethics – how to behave toward others.
Know presenting skills – how to communicate.

Wesley also taught that while a person is **TRANSFORMED** *by* the Holy Spirit, they are also **TRAINED** *with the assistance* of the Holy Spirit. We're not alone in the process of personal development or in the development of others. Leadership development and/or personal formation (discipleship) is a process that the Holy Spirit is very much involved in.

Whether it's natural or acquired gifts, whether it's something you're born with, or something you develop, none of it, says Wesley, is to be compared to **the GRACE OF GOD**.

In fact, much of what we're learning about ministry and leadership reveals a convergence between scientific knowledge and biblical knowledge; a pulling together of special revelation and general revelation. Always, however, giving prominence to the process of sifting all through the filter of scripture.

Like Wesley, I do not attempt to pit special and general revelation against one another, but combine what we can learn from each in proper harmony.

When God reveals truths about himself in scripture, we call it "special" revelation, and when he reveals truths about himself through nature, we call it "general" revelation. When we seek to understand a particular topic, special revelation gives us various passages that we can organize and interpret while general revelation provides us with various concepts and conclusions. The task of systematic theology is to organize what we can learn from each of these on their own, and then combine them together to produce a final more comprehensive view on the topic. And so, as Augustine said, "faith seeks understanding" and so **"we plunder the Egyptians."**

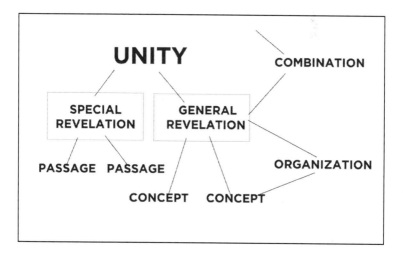

SELF-CONTROL, SELF-MANAGEMENT and SELF-LEADERSHIP LEAD TO CHARACTER, COMPETENCE AND CREDIBILITY

...and *SuperLeadership.*

While it begins with self-development, the goal is the development of others. Paul in Philippians 2:3-4 explains this by saying,

> "Do nothing out of selfish ambition or vain conceit. Rather, in humility value others above yourselves, [4] *not looking to your own interests but each of you to the interests of the others"* (NIV).

The implication is that personal interest is important. It is responsible behavior. But it is only one side of the servant leader coin. We MUST also have *other's* interests in mind— serving others is **THE KEY** to leadership in the Kingdom.

Serving others is the KEY to leadership in the Kingdom.

We addressed this question earlier, but I'd like to revisit it here, **"What is more important, character or competence?** Is it more important that one who aspires to lead be an honest, ethical person, who can be trusted, or a person who knows what they are doing; the quality or state of having sufficient knowledge, judgment, and skills?

If you've ever worked for, or with, someone who lacks either of these qualities; character or competence, then you know how frustrating it is.

And while it seems that character might be the simple and first answer, we also know that often competence in a certain field or endeavor can open the door for someone to be considered for a certain position.

I, therefore, prefer to take a "both-and" position in regard to the character-competence debate. I like to see it as **a two-sided coin that is spinning and difficult to tell one from the other.** Character and competence, working in a symbiotic relationship. We should not have to choose between these two important qualities. Both should be requirements. Anything less will result in some form of dysfunction and ineffectiveness.

So, character and competence working together, produce the all-important **CREDIBILITY** that is essential for leadership, especially Christian leadership. Because if they do not believe the messenger, they will not believe the message.

SUPERLEADERSHIP

Once the "character + competence = credibility" equation is fulfilled, then we move on to the all-important goal of **SUPERLEADERSHIP**.

This is a great label and concept—*SuperLeadership*. I wish I had come up with the term, but I can't take credit for it. I do, however, like it.

Charles Manz and Henry Sims (1989) conceived the idea of SuperLeadership as ***being the product and end goal* of individual self-leadership**. It is often described simply as, "leading others to lead themselves." SuperLeaders are expected to exemplify both strong self-leadership and high moral standards.

This is exactly what I see Jesus exemplified as he chose his disciples. His very first statement was, **"Come FOLLOW me"** (Mark 1:17).

It can be argued that the three most powerful *behavioral* words Jesus spoke were "COME, FOLLOW ME."

(Luke 18:22; see also Matt. 16:24; Mark 1:17; Luke 9:23).

FOLLOWERSHIP—it was the first criteria for leadership in the Kingdom.

"Come, follow me," Jesus said, "and I will send you out to fish for people" Matthew 4:19 (NIV).

The request was also the first lesson to learn of ***the primary mission within the Kingdom***—serving and reaching people.

SuperLeadership was the goal, but followership was the foundation of the developmental-formation process.

What could have inspired Peter to leave the safety of his boat in the middle of the Sea of Galilee during a boisterous storm? (Matthew 14:19). What led him to believe that if Jesus could walk on water, he could too? We can't know for certain, but perhaps Peter understood that the Son of God did not come just to do wonderful things ***for*** people but to ***empower people*** like Peter to do wonderful things too. Jesus sent a message to us all.

A ***SuperLeader*** is one who intentionally leads others to lead themselves by acting and serving as their coach, mentor and teacher. Paul understood the admonition and adopted it.

"Follow me as I follow Christ" (1 Corinthians 11:1). Paul says to his understudies, "Imitate me as I imitate Him."

SuperLeadership is about **paying it forward.** The simplest way to define this idea, is that *when someone does something for you, instead of paying that person back directly, you pass it on to another person instead.* The SuperLeader isn't looking to be paid back. He or she is looking for the *behavior* in you.

We see the challenge of SuperLeadership again as Paul challenges his protégé and us in 2 Timothy 2:1-2 (NLT) by saying,

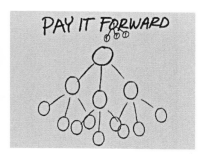

"You have heard me teach things that have been confirmed by many reliable witnesses. Now teach these truths to other trustworthy people who will be able to pass them on to others."

SuperLeadership within the ministry context is about **equipping the saints** (Ephesians 4:12). It's about **"shared leadership,"** collaboration and teamwork. Wow, talk about relevance and timeliness for today!

COLLABORATION is being referred to as "*THE* meta-skill of the 21st century. Then too, at SuperLeadership's CORE is servant leadership; leadership that models the way pursuing the 1 Corinthians 12 Body-of-Christ model; strength through diversity. It is a leadership model that appreciates each person's gift and contribution—it honors collaboration.

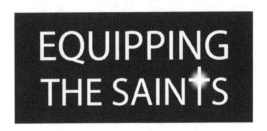

Albert Hubbard (1856-1915), an American writer, artist, and philosopher seems to have understood the value of this principle. Hubbard said,

> *"It's a fine thing to have ability, but the ability to discover ability in others is the true test."*

In this way, leaders are like locomotives. Locomotives are designed to pull trains. Leaders are designed to equip and empower *people* to become *leaders*.

**We start by modeling the way,
serving as an example.**

"**Follow my example as I follow the example of Christ.**"   (1 Corinthians 11:1)

Truth is,
true leaders don't create followers.
They create more leaders.

Let me paraphrase what Paul said in Ephesians 4:11-16,

"**Our responsibility is to equip God's people to do his work and build up the church, the body of Christ. [13] This will continue until we all come to such unity in our faith and knowledge of God's Son that we will be mature in the Lord, measuring up to the full and complete standard of Christ.**"

Before you are a leader,
success is all about
growing yourself.
When you become a leader,
success is all about
growing others.
--Jack Welch

I like to think of SuperLeadership as also incorporating several other models of leadership that provide interesting and challenging characteristics for the Christian leader to be aware of:

Situational Leadership (discussed earlier),
People-Centered Leadership,
Transformational Leadership,
and Servant Leadership.

*We will discuss these leadership models further in subsequent books in the 10 Essential Skills series.

I am fascinated by these models and extremely curious about them—I don't know of any other field of study like leadership that presents a greater variety of ideas for us to consider and grapple with, especially when it comes to doing our job better—to serve people in an enhanced manner.

Two thought leaders most impacted my development when it comes to understanding and appreciating various models and ways of thinking about something.

Renown psychologist and organizational theorist, **Kurt Lewin** (1952) said, **"There is nothing more practical than a good theory."**

Lewin's optimistic message was twofold. Theorists should first try to **provide new ideas** for understanding or thinking about a problematic or challenging situation. Second, hopefully these new ways of thinking will suggest potentially useful **new possibilities** for dealing with the situations.

Mary Jo Hatch, in her book on **Organizational Theory**, has been extremely influential in my understanding of leadership as well. She says, "if we are ever to realize the value of theory for practice, then we must master the use of multiple perspectives." She was encouraging thought leaders, especially academicians, to stay out of the "ivory tower" and provide ideas that are applicable in the real world. It is my hope as well that these distinctive perspectives will broaden our intellectual horizons, serve to stimulate our imagination, and increase our capacity to lead.

Chasing the rabbit of leadership models and theory will help you develop and think about leadership in a way that challenges your personal behavior and the ways organizations are led—ministry and church leadership is no exception. If we are to be Issachar leaders (1 Chronicles 12:32), "understanding *our* times and knowing what the church should to," then we must apply ourselves to advice like this.

PEOPLE-CENTERED LEADERSHIP

Ken Blanchard, best-selling author and chief spiritual officer of the Ken Blanchard Companies, refers to these *SuperLeaders* as **"People-Centered Leaders."** People-centered leaders draw out the best in people around them via coaching, mentoring and intentionally serving as an example.

According to Blanchard, it's not *just* about results. Results are important (even in the church). But **it's about people and results—in that order—people first**. It's about taking care of your people through meaningful connections and relationships; giving praise, support, and care—investing in them.

There is also the **transformational model of leadership**. This model likewise provides us with interesting challenges and clarifications about leadership that can assist us in our ministry of service to others.

TRANSFORMATIONAL
LEADERSHIP
BEHAVING RIGHTLY

Transformational leadership is defined as **a leadership approach that encourages change in individuals and in social systems**. In its ideal form, it creates valuable and positive change in followers with the end goal of developing followers into leaders. The transformational leader works with individuals and teams, encouraging behavior beyond their immediate self-interests.

Most credit the concept of transformational leadership to leadership author and researcher, **James MacGregor Burns** (1970s), who defined the actions of transformational leadership as "when one or more persons engage with others in such a way that leaders and followers raise one another to higher levels of motivation and morality."

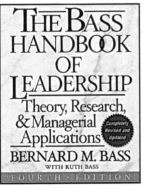

James MacGregor Burns is said to have inspired Bernard M. Bass (1925-2007), leadership researcher and professor, to expand upon the transformational leadership model. The *Bass Handbook of Leadership* has been described as "*the* authoritative resource book in the field of leadership, the indispensable 'bible' for every serious student of leadership."

In 1985, **Bernard M. Bass**, expanded on Burns' ideas to develop the **Bass Transformational Leadership Theory**, consisting of four main components of transformational leadership:

THE FOUR COMPONENTS OF TRANSFORMATIONAL LEADERSHIP

1. **Inspirational Motivation:**
   Imparting a vision that is appealing and worthy. Transformational leaders do that by communicating a vision so well, that followers internalize it and make the goal of achieving that vision their own.

2. **Individualized Consideration:**
   Concern for the professional development of people and fostering positive relationships with them. This involves keeping lines of communication open, attending to the individual needs of employees and staff, mentoring them and recognizing each person's unique contributions.

3. **Intellectual Stimulation:**
   Removal of the "fear factor."
   Empowers people to constantly be learning, looking for and acting upon opportunities, rather than playing it safe — what authors, **Kouzes and Posner** refer to as **"challenging the process,"** taking informed risks. Transformational leaders challenge assumptions and question the "this is the way we've always done things" mentality, taking on status quo assumptions.

4. Idealized Influence:
Transformational leaders serve as role models for employees and team members in every way. This also includes modeling ethical and socially desirable behavior. The foundation of this influence is trust and respect. With this trust, employees become followers who want to emulate their leaders and internalize their ideals.

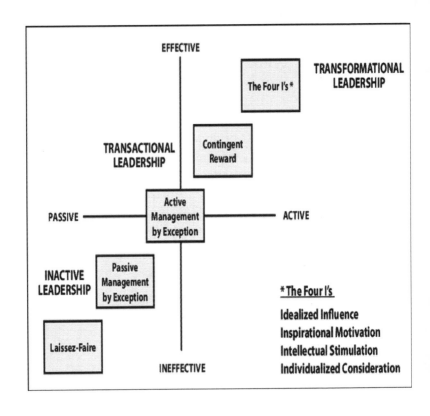

The Transformational Leadership Model
depicting the *"range of leadership."*

SERVANT LEADERSHIP

Robert K. Greenleaf (1904-1990) was the founder of the modern servant leadership movement and the Greenleaf Center for Servant Leadership. Greenleaf published a book entitled ***The Servant as Leader***, (1970). His book started a national and international discussion bringing to the forefront a principle taught in scripture for thousands of years. The ideas behind servant leadership are, indeed, ancient.

The bible only uses the term leader a few times. The term is used sparingly in scripture. In fact, when scripture refers to great men/women in the bible, the term "servant" is often used— "Moses my servant" and "Joshua my servant."

No one demonstrated and taught this better than Jesus. He taught we should be shareholders in other people's lives. Interestingly, one leadership article encouraged this idea, the celebration and development of others, at a 5 to 1 ratio.

The 5 to 1 Ratio

As you will see in the Servant Leadership book within this series, I refer to Servant Leadership by also calling it 20/20 Leadership. Primarily because the Servant Leader model is prescriptively taught by Jesus in Matthew 20 beginning in verse 20 (context is important). The passage, I believe, also brings the idea of

Servant Leadership versus *"top-down, command and control"* leadership into **FOCUS**.

In **Matthew 20:20–28** Jesus provides an explicit *prescriptive* template regarding leadership within the ministry context. He describes the secular leadership model with words like "exercising authority over you," "lording it over you," but quickly provides the directive **"not so with you."** Ken Blanchard refers to it as "not so with you" leadership. Jesus then describes the Kingdom model of servant leadership. He gives place for positional and legacy ambition, but cautions about the motivation of the heart.

People-centered Leadership—
SuperLeadership—
Transformational Leadership—
Situational Leadership, and
Servant Leadership,
all unleash the power and potential
of people for the greater good.

Don't just Identify Potential

Unleash it.

SECTION 4

BOTTOM LINE: YOU HAVE TO DO THE WORK

IT'S YOUR CHOICE

I have good news and bad news.
Which one do you want first?

BAD NEWS. *You have made the choices that have gotten you to where you are today.*

GOOD NEWS. *You have made the choices that have gotten you to where you are today.*

Everything in your life is a reflection of a choice you have made. If you want a different result, make a different choice.

Eleanor Roosevelt (1884-1962), served as the first lady of the United States from 1933 to 1945, during her husband President Franklin D. Roosevelt's four terms in office, making her the longest-serving first lady of the United States. President Harry S. Truman referred to her as the "First Lady of the World." Eleanor said there was "a ***link between personal philosophy and action***—one's behavior."

> "One's philosophy is not best expressed in words; it is expressed in the *choices* one makes. In the long run, we shape our lives and we shape ourselves. The process never ends until we die. And the *choices* we make are ultimately our own responsibility."
>
> Eleanor Roosevelt

I have routines. You have routines. We all have routines. Whether it's the way we start our days, commute to work, go to bed, or anything in between, we all have a certain way of doing things. Geniuses, both ancient and modern, tend to live and die by their routines—choices made so often that they've become "predictable."

Routine, however, at times, has to change. Becoming the best version of yourself fundamentally involves change. We cannot mature or develop without change. What got us to where we are today, will not take us to where we're going. This often requires stepping out of our comfort zones and stepping up to something new—the unknown, the unfamiliar, the new. **This means losing some control.** Kurt Lewin, in his **3-stage change model**, "unfreeze, change, refreeze," rightly taught that once the change process begins, personally or organizationally, it required a transition phase of disorganization and lowered effectiveness. Change requires adjustment.

So, here's the truth—much of this thing we call leadership, is, in fact, "out of control," because fundamentally leadership is about leading change—about adapting. The task and challenge of any leader is learning how to "be out of control, comfortably."

> # The task of the leader is to be "out of control, comfortably."

LIFE-LONG LEARNING

Personal development and formation require learning new insights, not just acquiring new information, but actually changing behaviors.

Scholars with the **Center for Creative Leadership** in Greensboro, North Carolina, say that "all development is self-development," and it is NEVER something done to us. And that if we neglect the *personal commitment* part of the development equation, development will cease. In fact, it will never get started in the first place without **PERSONAL COMMITMENT.**

The best development and training programs teach people how to be **LIFELONG LEARNERS**. Keeping up the brain's machinery for learning is vital for becoming and sustaining the best version of ourselves.

Here's the cold, hard truth—when you stop the learning, you stop the machinery. Unless you work on it, and are intentional about it, brain fitness begins declining around the age of 30 for men; a little longer for women. And don't ever mistake being active or busy for continuous learning.

The machinery is ONLY activated and maintained by LEARNING.

Learning how to learn, in terms of leadership, begins with the understanding that you need to seek out information about *your* leadership and *your* impact on others. How are you "showing up?" Be intentional about searching for information pertaining to your giftings, strengths, and core competencies. Be constantly on the lookout for information relevant to your job, position, and ministry. And especially look for competencies and skills benchmarked for that specific position.

I have three university degrees and everything I learned during my academic marathon simply and fundamentally prepared me for <u>continuous learning</u>.

Much of what we learn has a **SHELF LIFE**, with *social content* on the internet having relevance for approximately three hours. Truth is, we don't know what we don't know. And a critical aspect of self-awareness is realizing that you also have to learn enough about *YOURSELF* if you are to lead others.

Where then, do we encounter experiences that teach us these necessary realities? **Consider this:**

> **Research says that, "a leadership development program, like LeaderLabs, may be the only sustained time in a person's entire adult working life that they take a serious look at themselves."**

Leadership is often described as **getting the most out of other people**. I'd like to turn this assumption on its head and say instead that **authentic leadership begins with personal mastery.** Therefore, *the first job of leadership is to get the best out of yourself* and greater insight into yourself leads to greater insight to other people.

LEADERSHIP *is often*
described as
GETTING THE MOST
out of *Other People*
But, authentic leadership starts
with personal mastery.

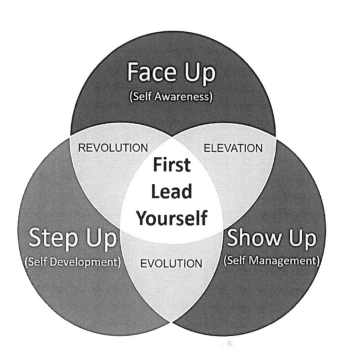

It has been said that the average person spends 98% of their life within their comfort zone.
But life outside your comfort is the zone where the magic happens.

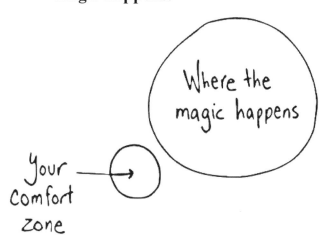

Change of any kind involves movement from a known but undesirable state to a desired but unknown state. The uncomfortable part involves a transition stage—stepping away from your comfort zone. It involves intentionally moving from what is known, to something unknown. It's the unknown of the future state that keeps a lot of people, organizations, and ministries, stuck in their present dysfunctional state. It's the **FEAR** that what's "out there" could possibly be worse than what is being experienced now.

Mark Sanborn said it perfectly, *"You need to disrupt your present thinking and refocus on what is important. Disrupt yourself before someone or something else does."*

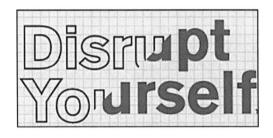

"Disrupt yourself before someone or something else does."

WE ARE NOT IN KANSAS ANYMORE

Truly, as Dorothy said to Toto in the Wizard of Oz, *"We're not in Kansas anymore."* Churches now (post-COVID) face a challenge that is more urgent and radical than it has been for many generations.

There are now major storm centers through which churches and their leaders must navigate, not in order to return to a previously more tranquil world, but to enter an entirely new one—referred to as **"the church on the other side."**

In the past, a leader could pull a prescription for a problem, challenge, or question off the shelf—well-worn ideas that worked for that time. But diversity and complexity have changed all this. There are, to be sure, still, a few problems and scenarios where a "quick fix" or someone's anecdotal advice might fit. But you better be sure and very careful.

Today, leaders have to think before acting—more than ever before.

According to Dr. Ellen Langer, Professor of Psychology at Harvard University.

> "When we confuse the stability of our mindsets with the stability of the underlying phenomenon, we act as if we know. When you think you know, you don't pay attention any longer—why should you—since you

know? But since things are always changing, uncertainty should be the rule, and you, as a leader, have to learn how to exploit the power in uncertainty."

THREE IMPORTANT WORDS + FOUR MORE

S O L U T I O N

In the past, anyone who had reached some level of leadership success—anyone who had climbed the ladder of the corporate or ministry food chain—was expected to display, among other things, an evident amount of **certainty and self-confidence**. In short, you're supposed to be **the person with all the answers**. But now, thinking of yourself like this, and behaving like this, can be a big mistake.

Today, the three words, *"I don't know"* constitute a powerful answer that shows humility and self-confidence. If you "bluff," attempt to act like the person with all the answers, and you're wrong, you will damage both your credibility and authenticity.

YOU DON'T NEED TO HAVE ALL THE ANSWERS
"I don't know" constitutes a powerful answer that shows humility and self-confidence.

When a leader is faced with a challenge they've never encountered before, it's okay not to know how to handle it. Admitting you don't have the answers is a lot better than pretending you do. Wouldn't you prefer a physician say *This type of surgery isn't my specialty. Let's find someone who is an expert on this matter to assist* rather than him *wing it* in fear of looking weak or not in control?

In these scenarios, admitting you need assistance or that you rely on someone else's expertise isn't a weakness. Instead, it shows the power of collaboration and your ability to build a strong, diverse team. It actually builds your credibility.

There is also another side of the "you don't have to have all the answers" advice. Just admitting that you don't know isn't enough. **What you say and do** is what will define you as a leader. Immediately after saying, "I don't know," you should say, "But, **together**, we will look for an answer. *I don't know, let's figure it out*" represents the three important words, plus four more.

Be careful though, a good leader should be good at knowing what they *don't* know and the words, "*I don't know*" should never be used as an excuse for incompetence. Problem is, many organizations and ministries suffer from what has been labeled **"The Peter Principle."**

In 1969 **Lawrence Peter** conducted research that exposed a dysfunctional behavior within most organizations. Peter's research was used in a book entitled, *"The Peter Principle."*

The book, was intended to be a satire. But it became popular because it actually made a serious point and called out a dysfunction of how people are too often promoted within hierarchical organizations. The principle describes how people within a certain organization **tend to rise to "a level of respective incompetence."** In other words, employees and team members are promoted based on their success in a previous job until they reach a level at which they are no longer competent. **The reality is, the skills that made you successful in one job, often do not**

translate to another job, position or context. And add insult to this injury with the fact that most organizations DO NOT provide adequate training for the new position. This is precisely why I refer to it as "the deep end of the pool," "sink or swim" leadership development program. **This is also why many people, after serving 18 or more months in a new position, would gladly return to their previous position, if they had the chance.**

Consequently, leaders *should* know, what their strengths are, especially if it's a core competency or key performance indicator of the job.

This is why the replies, "let me get back to you on that" or "I will find out more" are useful responses. (And if a decision needs to be made quickly, a leader can at least acknowledge what they *don't* know as part of their decision.)

The **"I don't know, but we'll find out"** course of action is what highly effective leaders do and by doing so they create a culture of ownership and **radical candor**.

THE IMPORTANCE OF VULNERABILITY AND COURAGE

Brene Brown, best-selling author, researcher and academic, shares her popular teachings on vulnerability and courage, declaring that when we dare drop the armor that protects us from feeling vulnerable, we open ourselves and others to experiences that bring purpose and meaning.

According to Brown, vulnerability is the key.

> **"Vulnerability is the willingness to show up and share your authentic self while knowing that you have no control over the outcome of your interactions."**

Thus, Brown, encourages normalizing the discomfort of learning and reframing failure as learning.

Michelangelo so aptly stated, **"The greatest danger for most of us is not that our aim is too high and we miss it, but that it is too low and we reach it."**

Therefore, self-starting. personal accountability, personal initiative, and personal agency are four principal competencies that must be considered and honed, IF a leader is to realize their personal best. But at the end of the day, it all comes down to one thing... **you've got to want it**.

Nike continues to use their famous tagline across much of their advertising and branding strategies. Nike says, "'**Just Do It**' is still as relevant to us today as it was decades ago."

Whether you view it as an **inspirational rallying cry** or **a bullying command,** the slogan 'Just Do It' is hard to avoid in modern life.

Accompanied by the familiar Nike swoosh, it appears on bags, T-shirts and billboards all over the world. As a statement it sums up the sports brand: it is competitive, forceful, direct, as lean and powerful as the athletes that appear alongside it in Nike's ads.

YOU HAVE TO DO THE WORK.

The implication? *"You have to do the work."* The statement represents the lion's share of productivity advice you'll ever need. Work is hard and people will latch onto anything to avoid doing the work.

It has been said that one of the most annoying phenomena in getting things done is that ***ideas have bad timing.*** Just try to stay focused on something. You finally get around to working on that project you've been saying you were going to work on. And all of a sudden, you're tormented by ideas—and you're distracted once again.

 In the best-selling book, *"Good to Great,"* **Jim Collins** puts forth what has become both a popular quote and inspirational theme, ***"Good is the enemy of great."***

The concept describes how too many people and too many organizations and/or ministries "settle" and take short cuts accepting that "good" is good enough and that they don't need to do the really hard work to be great. Being *just good* is the enemy of being great.

On the other hand, the statement can be seen to imply that we allow certain distractions to steal our focus and take away our attention from that which would be better defined as something "greater."

"good" IS THE *ENEMY* OF GREAT

To this end, **Peter Drucker** reminds us that the best decision makers know **when to say _NO_**. Drucker (1909–2005), argued strongly that **the most important ability of any leader was: Learning to say _NO_.** Learning how to say no may be the most valuable response we can arm ourselves with today.

The story is told of a distinguished psychologist who once reached out to Peter Drucker requesting an interview. Drucker responded by saying that he appreciated the offer but would have to disappoint him. Drucker responded by saying,

"One of the secrets of my productivity is to have a big waste paper basket to take care of all invitations such as yours."

Drucker was also known for being very direct. Fact is, a chief reason why Drucker was able to turn down such enticing offers was because he was passionately driven by his own work and knew the importance of prioritizing and saying "_NO._"

Another inspirational quote that speaks to this issue says, "Inspiration does exist, but it must find you working."

Another famous quote says, "Show up, show up, show up, and after a while the muse shows up, too." The inspiration and creativity will show up AS YOU WORK.

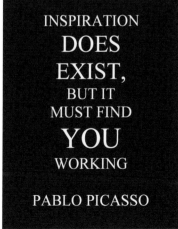

INSPIRATION **DOES EXIST,** BUT IT MUST FIND **YOU** WORKING

PABLO PICASSO

FOCUSED WORK WITH PURPOSE

We live in a time of constant crisis but these times are also pregnant with tremendous opportunities. And greater focus is crucial if we're to make the most of the extraordinary opportunities ahead.

Amos 9:13-15, speaks of a time when,

> "Things are going to happen so fast your head will swim; one thing fast on the heels of the other. You won't be able to keep up. Everything will be happening at once—and everywhere you look, blessings!"

 I believe we live in this reality NOW. It's a **"Yin and Yang"** type of season. Constant crisis and tremendous opportunity, complimentary forces, when seen through the lens of scripture.

"In the last days, perilous times will come" (2 Timothy 3:1) and Acts 2:17 adds, "'In the last days, God says, I will pour out my Spirit on all people."

We cannot afford to let this season of opportunity and potential slip through our fingers. Perilous times represent THE SIGN of unprecedented opportunity. We must be prepared. We must do the work.

We've already talked a great deal about this thing called **"potential."** Earlier I said "there is nothing more common than unsuccessful people with talent—with potential." And we, therefore, more often than not, talk about potential in the past tense, as something someone *had* but never realized.

When we say "people have potential," we conjure up mental images of people walking around with metaphorical *potential* buckets. And if yours is filled, then wherever you go, whatever you do, you have more opportunities to learn, grow, and be effective than those who have a less filled *potential* bucket.

"There is nothing more common than unsuccessful people with talent— with potential."

YOUR PERSONAL POTENTIAL BUCKET

If your bucket is full, then you're a "high potential,"—a **HiPo**. If your bucket is less filled with potential – or even not filled at all – you're called a **LoPo**, or a **NoPo**. As you can probably guess, it's not a great label to be saddled with.

There is a problem with this type of thinking. If you look at the data, you realize that **we've never been able to measure potential**.

Think about it. How awful is it to cloister opportunity off to an elite few, while preventing others from seeing everything that they *could be*? We can't reliably say that one person has more potential than any other person. All of us have the ability to learn and grow (it's a fact). We all, therefore, have potential.

The question is,

> "What will we do with it?"
> "Will we develop it?"
> "To what extent will we develop it?"

The One Thing That Levels the Playing Field

The #1 reason people don't reach their true potential: **they are unwilling to pay the price**. Many people don't want to invest their time or resources in order to grow themselves. And they do not join forces with others in order to help accelerate their growth.

Work means sitting down, focusing, putting pen to paper (or whatever) and doing it. It means taking action over a prolonged period of time. No amount of productivity hacking will make that easier.

I have read a lot of biographies and they generally have two things in common. First, they are obsessed about the work, and second, they never stray from *doing the work*. They are busy doing the work and guarding themselves from distractions that would take them away from the work. They stay busy doing the work until *that* work is completed. Then and only then do they move on to other work.

You have to find a way to block every possible distraction. You have to figure out what is the "greatest good." What is your most important project and goal? Then, you **just do the work**.

You can do this!

The implications of bad and poor leadership are staggering. Great leaders can be made. And the Holy Spirit will partner with us on this journey. Make no mistake, it's no accident, we are here for "such a time as this."

The next book in this series examines information discussed in LAB #1, Integrity of Heart.

The Bible teaches that what we say and do, and who we become, is the result of the state of our heart. Biblical writers use the heart to highlight the core of a person where thoughts, feelings, desires, and choices begin. This is why God examines the heart because He sees into the inner motivations of our heart. And this is why character development is foundational to Christian leadership development and formation.

I look forward to our continued journey of personal development and formation. It is an exciting journey.

WE NEED LEADERS.

35 THINGS YOU WILL LEARN FROM LEADERLABS

1. Why complete honesty is the #1 leadership characteristic.
2. Why understanding yourself is the #1 prerequisite for personal growth.
3. Learn why self-management is more important than time-management.
4. Learn why INITITATIVE is the introductory step to *effective* leadership.
5. Why ministers need to actually learn to SERVE; not be served.
6. Learn the true meaning of responsibility – response-able.
7. Learn about the #1 mistake leaders make and how to fix it.
8. Understand what top leaders are doing when at their extraordinary best.
9. Understand the three stages and eight steps to every change initiative.
10. Learn how to create conflict positive environments - conflict management. Prevent 50-75% of conflict.
11. Learn the top 4 words in conflict management.
12. Discover your purpose and develop mission, vision and core values.
13. Develop a personal development plan for second adulthood.
14. Learn the importance of and how to empower a team.
15. Learn habits to adopt if you "for real" want to change the world.
16. Learn how to stop procrastination.
17. Learn how to live in the quadrant of the important instead of the urgent.
18. Learn the art of focus and priority.
19. Learn to live life intentionally versus "Que Será Será."
20. Get to know the you that everyone else knows; uncover your blind spots.
21. Understand the principle of HIRE SLOW, and when to FIRE FAST.

22. Learn why "IT DEPENDS" is Dr. Garmon's two favorite words.
23. Learn the two top questions to ask before leading any change initiative.
24. Learn why "isolation" is worse than obesity and smoking.
25. Understand why you should never be the smartest person in the room.
26. Understand the science behind shutting the back door-developmental levels.
27. Learn the importance of life-long learning and how to love it.
28. Understand the meaning behind the saying, "All things are created twice," – mental and physical.
29. Learn what SuperLeadership is and how to be a SUPER-LEADER.
30. Learn the answer to the question, "What would you do if you weren't afraid?"
31. Learn how to become "The best version of yourself."
32. Learn how to read five books every month; and like it.
33. Learn how to "Order your private world."
34. Learn what to say "no" to.
35. Learn the leadership characteristic that is twice as important as Intelligence Quotient (IQ).

WWW.LEADERLABS.COM

leaderLABS 2.0

10 SKILLS
SELF-LEADERSHP &
SELF-MANAGEMENT

10 SKILLS
PERSONALITY
GETTING TO KNOW THE YOU EVERYONE ELSE KNOWS

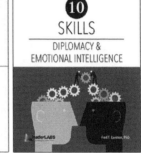

10 SKILLS
DIPLOMACY &
EMOTIONAL INTELLIGENCE

10 SKILLS
TO CREATE A CONFLICT
POSITIVE ENVIRONMENT

10 SKILLS
MANAGING YOUR CONNECTIONS
THE LONELINESS EPIDEMIC AND
THE EXISTENTIAL IMPORTANCE OF RELATIONSHIPS

10 SKILLS
THE JOHARI WINDOW
TO SEE AND ACKNOWLEDGE YOUR BLIND SPOTS

THESE 8 LABS COVER THE MOST ASKED QUESTIONS AND OBSERVATIONS FROM THE FIRST "TEN ESSENTIAL SKILLS" PROGRAM.

10 SKILLS
TIME & PRIORITY
MANAGEMENT

10 SKILLS
SELAH
SILENCE & SOLITUDE
THE EXISTENTIAL NECESSITY TO PAUSE, REFLECT, AND THINK

leaderLABS 3.0

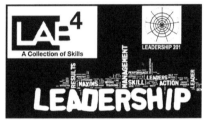

COMPETENCY BASED TRAINING

Snapshot of the
10 Essential Skills

1) Integrity of Heart

Character & Credibility

Character and credibility are essential components of integrity, the foundation for trust; integrity is the number one leadership characteristic followers look for in their leaders. The Bible explains how imperative this trait is by declaring, "Above all else, guard your heart" (Proverbs 4:23).

A leadership crisis marks both the marketplace and the ministry: a crisis of character and competence. Steven Covey described it as a move from a character ethic to a personality ethic.

Christian leaders are called above all else to be people of character. People want above all else leaders of character. Character is the foundation of leadership.

2) Self-Awareness

Looking in the mirror

Also understood as "looking in the mirror," self-awareness or self-perception is the absolute fundamental prerequisite of effective leadership. This essential skill requires leaders to learn about themselves in order to lead others. Self-perception may be different than the perception of others.

The leader must come to grips with and learn to resolve internal conflicts —dissonant internal chords. This distinctive is called "harmonious leadership," where you are "in tune" internally. You cannot lead others until you first lead yourself through a struggle with opposing values.

3) Servant Leadership

Descending into greatness

This skill takes a biblically counter-intuitive approach toward leadership aimed at "descending into greatness" rather than climbing the proverbial ladder of success. Jesus' prescriptive teaching on leadership in the Matthew 20:20, "not so with you," leadership model cautioned against leadership styles that "lorded it over" and "exercised authority over" people. The self-promoting/self-protecting leader contrasts strongly with the humble leader who displays confidence in God (Philippians 2).

The Christian leader has no Option B or C. Servant leadership is the only attitude and style to be pursued and adopted.

4) Situational Leadership

Learning to juggle styles

Research indicates that the biggest mistake leaders make is attempting to lead everyone the same way. This word of wisdom implies that a leader should have more than one leadership style in her/his leadership toolbox and must know how to juggle those styles. Effective leaders lead by using different styles (directing, coaching, supporting, delegating), and matching that style to the developmental level of their followers.

5) Transformational Leadership

Champions of Change

The best leaders are not the ones that issue orders; rather they use transformational leadership because it champions valuable and positive change in the individuals with the end goal of developing followers into leadership. Transformational leaders connect their followers' sense of identity and self to the mission and the collective identity of the organization. They are idealized in the sense that they are moral exemplars working toward the benefit of the team, organization and/or community.

6) Leading Change

Navigating Uncertainty

80-85% of churches in America are plateaued and/or in decline. The main reason? They don't know how to deal with spiraling, complex change. The speed of change was once defined as incremental, but today terms such as white-water, bullet-train and light-speed now describe change. Navigating uncertainty has become an essential leadership aptitude. Many leaders are struggling in this unsettled environment, mainly because they don't know how to deal with spiraling, complex change. Research and experience indicate that change has three fundamental stages and nine components, all of which can be learned.

7) Leading Conflict

Creating Conflict Postive Environments

Thousands of pastors in the USA leave ministry every year primarily due to mismanaged conflict. Conflict is a lot like water—it spills over, it flows downhill, and—if left unchecked—it erodes whatever it touches. And sometimes it's like red wine: it stains.

It's important to remember that several styles/modes may be used in conflict situations, but each person tends to habitually use a certain style more than others. To most effectively resolve a conflict, a leader should use the style/strategy most appropriate for the particular conflict situation. However, that strategy may not be the strategy that he/she habitually uses.

Skill 7 is, therefore, intentionally called "leading" conflict versus "managing" it because a leader must learn to understand and get ahead of conflict by creating "conflict positive environments." This is accomplished by understanding several things about oneself and conflict itself, different styles of conflict, how to use these styles in different contexts, and managing rational and personal conflict issues.

8) Water You Swim In

Vision, Values, & Culture

The question is asked, "What does a fish think about the water it swims in?" Answer: "It doesn't." It's the same with organizational values, vision and culture. Organizational culture is represented by the values and behaviors that contribute to the unique social and psychological environment of the organization.

Skill 8 is critical to Skills 9 and 10 that follow. If there is no clear vision (built upon shared values, mission and purpose) the resulting misalignment of direction and motivation will make the development of leaders difficult, if not impossible.

A leader cannot lead effectively without being crystal clear on the questions—Why are we here? and Where are we going?

In addition, people use their values to make decisions, but they rarely analyze their values and often make decisions for reasons they do not fully understand. Becoming aware of their values should improve their decision-making. People also prefer to associate with others who share their values. Thus, understanding values allows people to manage their relationships more effectively.

9) The Road Ahead

A Personal Development Plan

We live in a time of continual learning, growth and development. A leader must be continually learning and managing their personal knowledge base. Where do you see yourself in a year, five years —and perhaps ten years down the road? A personal development plan will help figure that out, and help you get there.

Today's environment stresses continual life-long learning. Personal growth and development is therefore a process. Intentionally designing and implementing a personal development plan is fundamentally important to present and future success. Winston Churchill said, "He who fails to plan is planning to fail."

10) Developing a Bench

A team development plan

Godly protégés are the leader's legacy. The gospel is always one generation from extinction. A team development plan is critical. Credible and competent protégés represent the leader's legacy. Every leader should intentionally have several people over them whom the leader is learning from and several people under them whom they are intentionally mentoring.

Teamwork has become the norm in organizational and ministry life; therefore, investing in and understanding team development has become increasingly important.

Many organizations today are complex, and so are many working teams. Virtual teams, cross-cultural teams, cross-functional teams, temporary project teams and teams that span a range of organizations are now standard. Team development planning is core to organizational development.

Teamwork skills are used to enhance understanding, communication and productivity. Developing self-awareness and shared awareness through assessment, feedback and coaching is a great start. An effective team must learn how to make giving and receiving feedback the normal way of improving cohesion and performance. They must also know how to use conflict as a constructive force, while also helping team members to know when to take the lead and when to enable others to lead.

The single biggest factor determining whether a team is cohesive or not is the leader. The leader must be out front, not as a cheerleader or figurehead, but as an active tenacious driver of teamwork.

Thank you for reading "Foundations for Self-Leadership."

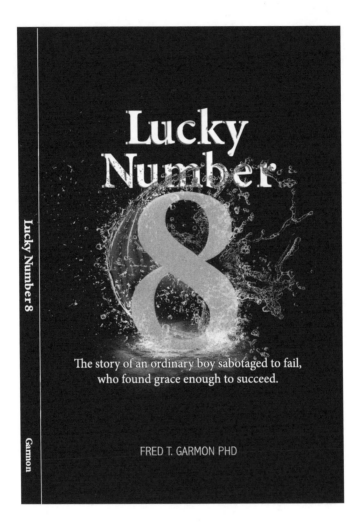

Check out Dr. Garmon's book, "Lucky Number 8" where he shares his life-changing testimony. Available on Amazon and on our website www.leaderlabs.com.